Paper Boats In The Monsoon

LIFE IN THE LOST WORLD OF ANGLO-INDIA

Owen Thorpe

2007

Order this book online at www.trafford.com/07-1056
or email orders@trafford.com

Most Trafford titles are also available at major online book retailers.

© Copyright 2007 Owen Thorpe
All rights reserved. No part of this publication may be reproduced, stored in a retrieval system, or transmitted, in any form or by any means, electronic, mechanical, photocopying, recording, or otherwise, without the written prior permission of the author.

Note for Librarians: A cataloguing record for this book is available from Library and Archives Canada at www.collectionscanada.ca/amicus/index-e.html

Printed in Victoria, BC, Canada.

ISBN: 978-1-4251-2965-1

We at Trafford believe that it is the responsibility of us all, as both individuals and corporations, to make choices that are environmentally and socially sound. You, in turn, are supporting this responsible conduct each time you purchase a Trafford book, or make use of our publishing services. To find out how you are helping, please visit www.trafford.com/responsiblepublishing.html

Our mission is to efficiently provide the world's finest, most comprehensive book publishing service, enabling every author to experience success. To find out how to publish your book, your way, and have it available worldwide, visit us online at www.trafford.com/10510

 www.trafford.com

North America & international
toll-free: 1 888 232 4444 (USA & Canada)
phone: 250 383 6864 ♦ fax: 250 383 6804 ♦ email: info@trafford.com

The United Kingdom & Europe
phone: +44 (0)1865 722 113 ♦ local rate: 0845 230 9601
facsimile: +44 (0)1865 722 868 ♦ email: info.uk@trafford.com

10 9 8 7 6 5 4 3

For Paddy

Who has shared my life's journey for over forty years—a wonderful travelling companion.

I remember a day in my childhood I
floated a paper boat in the ditch.
It was a wet day of July; I was alone
and happy over my play.
I floated my paper boat in the ditch.

Suddenly the storm clouds thickened,
Winds came in gusts, and rain poured
in torrents.
Rills of muddy water rushed and
swelled the stream and sunk my boat.
Bitterly I thought in my mind that
the storm came on purpose to spoil my happiness;
all its malice was against me.

The cloudy day of July is long today,
And I have been musing over all
those games in life wherein I was the loser.
I was blaming my fate for the many
tricks it played on me, when suddenly
I remembered the paper boat that sank
in the ditch.

The Gardener: No.70
Rabindranath Tagore

CONTENTS

Introduction 11
1. Who Are The Anglo-Indians? 17
2. A Chokra Childhood 31
3. Off To School 49
4. Feeding And Entertaining The Inner
   And Outer Chokra 63
5. Family Life 81
6. The Orphanage 111
7. The Prison Camp 125
8. A Round Trip To Delhi 145
9. Jesuits And Rock 'N' Roll 181
10. The Statesman 213
11. The Calcutta Scene 237
12. Blighty Bound 253
13. Welcome To London 261
14. What Happened Next? 269

Appendices:
A. The Tree 279
B. A Selection Of Suggested Reading 293

LIST OF ILLUSTRATIONS

1. Eric Thorpe and his brothers, Leonard, Owen and Richard. Eric, my father, is on the left.

2. Owen, Wensley, John and Susan Thorpe. Coimbatore 1955. Owen is on the left.

3. My parents, Marjorie and Eric. Coimbatore 1955.

4. My wedding, December 1968, cutting the cake.

5. Paddy and Owen out for the evening in Calcutta. I am trying on a moustache for size! 1969

6. The Fathoms. A publicity picture for performances at the Grand Hotel, Calcutta. 1963/4.

7. Mike, Man and Owen—my short-lived jazz/rock band. Mike is out of shot.

Cover: Street scene, Wellesley Tank, Calcutta from a painting by the Author.

Introduction

This book is a record of my memories of my life in India from the mid 1940s, just before India achieved Independence from the British Raj, to 1970 when I left for the UK—part of the great Anglo-Indian exodus—I haven't been back since. I originally wrote it as a bit of family history for my children and grandchildren, but then thought it might interest a wider audience, giving those of you who are Anglo Indians a remembrance of times past; those of you who are the children of Anglo-Indians, but born in the western world, some idea of the type of life your family lived in India—and for those of you who are new to the subject a peek into what it was like to be an Anglo-Indian growing up in India.

We Anglo-Indians, and by that term I mean people of mixed race, not the old British term for Brits born and resident in India, existed in a sort of bubble, living life on our own terms. Neither the British nor the Indians held us in the deepest regard because to them we were neither one thing or another, and we quickly learned to shrug off the derogatory names they threw at us: 'chi chis', 'half-castes', and so on. We regarded ourselves as proudly European, and we certainly did not consider ourselves to be Indians or Pakistanis. In many ways this was our strength as it made us fiercely independent and unwilling to compromise our way of life—we borrowed from both cultures and created something unique. It was also our weakness as we failed to integrate and pledge our allegiance to the country of our birth—our hearts and minds were committed elsewhere. This loyalty, however, was not reciprocated in Britain's abandonment of the community following Indian and Pakistani independence. We Anglo-Indians have responded, characteristically, by making our way independently to new lives in Australia, Canada the USA and even to Britain, breaking new ground as our forefathers did.

Despite our exodus there are ties that continue bind us—paradoxically, they now bind us more strongly to each other despite the distance. There are regular re-unions and regular requests over the Internet to trace school friends and work colleagues now dispersed around the world. We continue to cling strongly to our shared identity knowing that it is in danger of disappearing. There is that spark of instant recognition when two Anglo-Indian strangers meet: it can come from physical appearance—the coffee cream complexion, or the dark hair light skin combination; it can come from the echoes of a familiar inflexion in an accent—and the bond is made. Give it a few minutes and the conversation will go from a tentative, "Do you come from India/Pakistan?" to, "Yes, I remember so and so, I was at school with his brother." Connections are established, mutual friends identified, relatives even. And the conversation is an easy one—you cannot, for example, imagine two English people doing it. It is because, in those moments, there is an unspoken sharing of a history, experience, and the desire to identify with one another. It is an experience like no other.

In the natural course of events the community and its culture will slowly dilute as our children and grandchildren marry outside the community, pledge their allegiance to their new parent countries and take on the culture and aspirations of their new countrymen and women. Echoes of our Anglo-Indian past will continue in the family use of Indian words or expressions for certain situations or things[1]; in the stories told by the old

---

1   I used to tease my children by saying "bathi" and opening my fingers in a sunburst to get them put the light on—they have anglicised it to "batti."

and especially in the food we eat. This last may prove to be the most enduring link to our Anglo-Indian past—long live the *aloo chop*[1], ball curry and yellow rice, brinjal cutlets and *panthras*!

This is not meant to be a scholarly social history. Others have done the scholarly bit and there are references to their work in this book should you wish to know more. Mine is an ordinary life, typical of that lived by many Anglo-Indians in India or Pakistan. I was lucky enough to move around India and experience at first hand the Anglo-Indian communities in small-town Coimbatore in South India, Madras (which will never be Chennai to me), Delhi and Calcutta (Cal to those who lived there). I hope that you will find my story entertaining.

My own Anglo-Indian origins arise through my paternal grandmother, Minna Thorpe (nee Evans), who, from her dark complexion, was clearly of mixed race—probably Welsh and Indian. My grandfather, Horace Thorpe (really Horace Langridge) who married her was English and was born in East Sussex in England, joining the army and coming out to India in 1894. My mother's family, though they lived in India for generations, claimed never to have inter-married—they were of a

---

[1] The 'aloo chop' or potato cutlet is the signature Anglo-Indian dish. Made of spicy mince coated in mashed potato, rolled in breadcrumbs and fried.

group then known as 'domiciled Europeans'. My mother's people were a mixture of Scots and Irish, with a splash of French Huguenot[1] thrown in.

In writing this book I am indebted to my wife, Paddy, for her patience and forbearance. I would like to thank my brother Wensley for putting together the photographs in it. And to thank my builders, who forced me to escape into my study to do something productive while they tore bits of my house down before putting it together again.

Owen Thorpe
Banstead, Surrey
England
2007

---

1 The Huguenots were French Protestants, who fled a Catholic France where they were persecuted. Many were in the silk-weaving trade and settled in Spitalfields in the East End of London.

1

Who Are The Anglo-Indians?

Though I did promise this wasn't a scholarly work, I think it is important to know how the Anglo-Indians came to be. A short history of the Anglo-Indians goes something like this:

The East India Company, granted a Royal Charter by Queen Elizabeth I on 31 December 1600 to trade in the East Indies, encouraged, in 1687, legitimate marriages between its British employees and native women. It even offered a gold Pagoda (a high value coin) as an inducement. The reason for this was simple: the climate and harsh conditions in India caused high mortality among Europeans and it took six months to get replacements out of England because they had to come by sea round Africa and the treacherous Cape of Good Hope as the Suez Canal was not yet built. By encouraging the children of local unions, the East India Company could create a stock of ready employees who, because they were native born, were more able to survive the local conditions and would have the European language and culture as well as understand the native language. The Portuguese had pioneered the way in 1510 when the Portuguese Governor of India, Alfonso d'Albuquerque, encouraged his countrymen to marry Indian women in order to establish Portuguese authority in India. The offspring of these mixed marriages between the Portuguese and Indians were known as Luso-Indians.

Many of the East India Company staff, starved of female company as women were generally forbidden from travelling on the Company's ships, naturally became interested in and formed liaisons with the local women—sometimes by arrangement with their families, or by forming attachments with battlefield widows or with slave girls and camp followers. These consorts, known as '*Bibis*,' were well provided for and the fairer children of the senior officers were sometimes sent home to England to be educated and prepared for posts in the East India Company—some never returned. These local liaisons continued well into the 17th and 18th Centuries but, though tolerated, the *Bibis* were never fully accepted in Indo-European society. The famous Col. James Skinner was the son of a Scots army officer who captured and married a Muslim *zamindar's* (land owner's) daughter. Sir David Ochterlony (1758—1825) had thirteen *Bibis* (how did he divide his time among them?) and a familiar sight in Delhi was of Ochterlony and the *Bibis* taking an evening stroll around the city, each *Bibi* on her own elephant.

In 1786, Lord Cornwallis succeeded Warren Hastings as Governor General in India. In contrast to Hastings, Cornwallis had no experience of India and arrived with the view that all Indians were corrupt. He replaced Hastings's policy of working cooperatively with the Indians for one that excluded them from the administration and armed forces. Every Indian official was removed from his post and he took steps to bar Anglo-Indians from the ranks of the military—though they could be bandsmen and farriers. He also barred them from the covenanted civil service. Living allowances for Anglo-Indian wives of soldiers were half that of allowances for European wives on the basis that the Anglo-Indians were "born in India and habituated to live chiefly on rice" and that their other needs were "more confined than those of a European woman"[1].

---

1   Archie Baron, An Indian Affair, from Riches to Raj. 2001

In the 1790s, there was a mulatto rebellion in the French colony of Haiti; this was used as an excuse to reduce the power and position of mixed race people. The mulattos, who were a mixture of whites and Negroes, were generally better educated than the indigenous Negroes, and sought to overthrow their French masters. This caused a fright around Europe because of the threat posed to their commercial interests. The East India Company's response was to issue a decree that, *"No person, the son of a native Indian, can be appointed to the civil, military or navy services".* This applied to all 'country borns' as the children of English/native liaisons had come to be called. These Anglo-Indians were immediately discharged from their jobs and forbidden from owning land or living more than 10 miles from an East India Company settlement.

This simply did not make sense in India because the Anglo-Indians were a deliberate hybrid designed, if you like, to embrace their European language, culture and customs. They were unlikely to side with the Hindus as they fell outside their rigid caste system, or with the Muslims because they were Christians and therefore infidels.

Though the East India Company was apt to conscript Anglo-Indians into the army in times of emergency, they were generally stood down once the emergency was over. They were not treated as equals and were subjected to harsher native Hindu/Muslim law rather than British law. Their legal position was challenged in the British Parliament in 1830 by John William Ricketts because Anglo-Indians were in the difficult position of not being recognised as either Indian or British and had no rights under British law. Many sons of European fathers and Indian mothers were forced to seek employment in the armies of the native princes because they could not become officers in the East India Company's or British armies.

Even that avenue was subsequently cut off by the British who, when they went to war with the Mahrattas declared that anyone working for the native princes would be regarded as a traitor. You can imagine the shock and crises of conscience that this caused among stalwart and loyal people who, through accident of birth, were being placed in an invidious position. There is a good personal account given by the splendid Col. James Skinner, who went on to found Skinner's Horse, the legendary regiment of irregular cavalry, of the turmoil at the time when the 'country born' officers, of whom he was one, decided that they could not go on serving the Mahratta princes in their war against the British. He says that a proclamation was made by the British "to all the British and country-born officers, late of Scindia's, (the Mahratta prince) that we should meet with punishment, if we were found again in arms against the British." Skinner very reluctantly decided to quit the Mahratta service—he had eaten their salt and they were his friends. Leading a group of country-born and European officers to join the British, they were poorly received in the British camp and Skinner nearly went back to the Mahrattas, but the situation was saved when a senior British officer recognised him—his name was already well known for his heroic exploits and as a highly skilled soldier—and made him and his companions welcome. It was a good thing that Skinner did not go back as some of his fellow country-born officers were horribly put to death by the peevish Mahratta princes—some of the most senior had their heads trampled on by elephants.[1]

In 1833 Parliament changed the East India Company Charter to remove its monopoly on trade in India and declared that British law would be applied equally to all. However, senior Company posts were still available for recruitment only in England, effectively preventing the Anglo-Indians from applying for them unless they had the means to get to England in the first place.

Also in 1833, the East India Company's ban on European women travelling on its ships to India was lifted, and in 1869 the opening of the Suez Canal made the journey to

---

[1] Military Memoinr of Lieut. Col. James Skinner, C.B. by J. Baillie Fraser Esq. 1856

India easier and quicker and brought more Europeans, including women, to India—the beginning of the notorious 'fishing fleet' of women seeking husbands. The Anglo-Indians found themselves displaced from senior and middle-ranking jobs. More importantly, because of the uptight Victorian morality that came with the arrival of a new breed of evangelical Company officers and then the arrival of the 'memsahibs', liaisons between Europeans and Indians and Anglo-Indians were now frowned upon. Anglo-Indians were forced into supporting roles in the railways, post and telegraph, police, customs etc.

Despite this very direct form of discrimination, Anglo-Indians distinguished themselves in support of the British Raj in the Indian Mutiny of 1857: examples are of Hearsey in Calcutta; the boys of La Martiniere School in Lucknow, who withstood the siege of Lucknow; the brave telegraph signallers, Brendish and Pilkington, in Delhi who stuck to their posts to signal the news of the mutiny at Meerut and the arrival of the mutineers in Delhi. There are also many accounts of individual acts of sheer heroism by 'Eurasians', both men and women, who suffered equally at the hands of the mutineers.

With Indian Independence in 1946, an Article in India's new Constitution (which carried over Article 366 (2) of The British Government of India Act 1935) officially defined an Anglo-Indian: *"An Anglo-Indian means a person whose father or any of whose other male progenitors in the male line is or was of European descent but who is domiciled within the territory of India or was born within such territory of parents habitually resident therein and not established there for temporary purposes only."* The mother's nationality, it seems, was totally irrelevant—perhaps the drafters of the Constitution could not bear to envisage a possible liaison between a European woman and an Indian or Anglo-Indian.

With Independence in 1947, the discrimination against Anglo-Indians intensified. Where previously they had been discriminated against by the British, they now found themselves discriminated against by the new Indian ruling elite, to whom they were an unwelcome by-product of the Raj. The British failed the community by not according them dual nationality as the Dutch had done for their Eurasian citizens. In order to gain British nationality, Anglo-Indians had to prove British nationality on their father's side. The British decided that they had done their bit for the Anglo-Indians by having included in the Indian Constitution provision for the community to be represented by two Members of Parliament.

The tragedy of the Anglo-Indians is that they were between the proverbial rock and a hard place—both the British and the Indians looked down on them. Anglo-

Indians were culturally British in their speech, dress and beliefs but they never seriously took to learning Indian languages and customs and almost defiantly failed to assimilate themselves as good Indian citizens. Their very names and their style of dress set them apart in post-Independence India. Because of a history of doubt and uncertainty about their futures theirs tended to be a 'live for today' culture. They were never really going to fit in after Indian independence.

Though many authors and even social scientists in the past have had derogatory things to say about the character of people of mixed race, they have only to look into their own historical backgrounds to see just how mixed their own ancestry was. The 'pure' English were a mixture of Jutes, Angles and Saxons from Germany, Vikings, Celts, Romans and Normans (who were also descended from the Vikings—the word Norman is derived from 'Norse man'). And what of the scientific research on DNA that has shown that we are all descended out of Africa? There was a recent programme on British television which examined the DNA of a number of people who had proclaimed themselves to be '100 per cent English'—I enjoyed their looks of shock and horror when it was revealed that they weren't. I like to think that the reaction to the Anglo-Indians arose out of a similar reaction to the revolt of the mulattos in Haiti—this hybrid community posed a threat. We may not have been in the positions of power and eminence, but we were the ones who knew how to operate the levers.

Even Rudyard Kipling, who did so much to open the mysteries of India to a European readership, was not immune from prejudice against the Anglo-Indians. In his book, Plain Tales from the Hills, he has a story called Kidnapped, which is about an Englishman called Peythroppe who caused a scandal when he fell in love with a mixed race girl—*"Miss Castries—d'Castries it was originally, but the family dropped the d' for administrative reasons."* He goes on to say, "It was obviously absurd that Peythroppe should marry her. The little opal-tinted onyx at the base of her fingernails said this as plainly as print." Kipling thus perpetuated, maybe even introduced the notion that you could tell an Anglo-Indian by looking at the colour of the half-moon at the base of their fingernails, even if they were fair-skinned. And how does Kipling's story end? Peythroppe was kidnapped by his European colleagues and so missed the day of his wedding to Miss Castries. Kipling concludes: *"One of these days he will marry; but he will marry a pink-and-white maiden..."* Despite his prejudices, Kipling's novel, Kim, remains for me one of the greatest and most perceptive books about Raj India—I re-read it at least every couple of years.

In any society, there are people who are at different points in the spectrum, from the rich and successful to the poor and destitute, good to the bad. There were Anglo-Indians who were the product of the liaisons of high born British families who benefited from their patronage and wealth. Others were descended from the liaisons of private soldiers of very limited means, and had to struggle accordingly. Of course there were bound to be differences, but the Victorian preoccupation with social status condemned the entire community to an inferior position. It didn't help that Anglo-Indians were forced into subordinate roles in the machinery of the Raj.

Anglo-Indians have emerged as a proud and resilient people. We can hold our own in this world having walked the tightrope between the Brits and the Indians, and we have demonstrated, through national and personal achievement, that we are inferior to no one. We follow some outstanding and inspirational people across all walks of life:

> **Colonel James Skinner**—founder, with his brother Robert, of Skinner's Horse, a distinguished cavalry regiment. A hero of mine.
>
> **William Linnaeus Gardner**—who founded Gardner's Horse.

Hyder Young (Jung) Hearsey—soldier and artist.

Field Marshal Lord Roberts VC—hero of the Indian Mutiny.

Lord Liverpool—Prime Minister 1812

William Pitt—Prime Minister

Henry Derozio—author and poet who played a significant role in some of the earliest attempts at the creation and definition of a modern Indian identity.

Flight Lieut Leefe Robinson VC—shot down the first Zeppelin over England

Wing Cmdr Guy Gibson VC—of the Dambusters

Orde Wingate—leader of the Chindit force which liberated Burma from the Japanese in WW II

Merle Oberon—Hollywood actress

Boris Karloff—Hollywood actor

John Masters—author

Sir Cliff Richard and Englebert Humperdinck—singers

Sir Ben Kingsley—actor

Vivien Leigh—actress

Anna Leonowens—the Anna of Anna and the King of Siam

Leslie Claudius, who captained India in hockey in four consecutive Olympics between 1948 and 1960 and won three gold medals and a silver. Many Anglo-Indians were members of the Olympic gold medal winning Indian hockey teams of the past.

And let's not forget the thousands of men and women in the civil administration, police, railways, post and telegraph, customs and excise, nursing and the armed services who helped build and support the British Raj in India, helped defend the British Empire across the globe and supported the shaky first steps of the newly independent India and Pakistan—and those who are now making names for themselves in their new countries.

2

A Chokra Childhood

We left Jhansi in the dead of night. My father dressed in unfamiliar mufti after years in the army, my mother struggling with her three small sons—Wensley, eight years old; me, three, and an infant John—and all of the family's belongings. We had locked up and left our army bungalow in the Jhansi cantonment that afternoon to kill time with our friends, the Pragers, before we caught the night train out. Mr Prager was obviously a keen *shikari*[2] from the number of stuffed animal heads and animal skins that decorated

---

2   Hunter

his sitting room—I was fascinated by the tiger skin rug, particularly the tiger's head and realistic glass eyes, as I'd never seen a tiger close up before. We had a long journey ahead of us, all the way south down the spine of India and then the short detour from Coimbatore Junction in the shadow of the Western Ghats, changing to the narrow gauge train at Mettupalayam for Ootacamund—Ooty—in the Nilgiri Hills. It was 1949, the post-war and post-Independence demobilisation of the armed services was well underway and my father had left the army to return to his pre-war career of teaching.

Jhansi, a town so memorable in the history of the Indian Mutiny of 1857 for the part played by Laxmibhai, the Rani of Jhansi, and for the siege of Jhansi fort and the infamous massacre of its 56 Europeans and Eurasians (18 men, 19 women and 19 children) by the mutineers who had falsely guaranteed them safe conduct. It was now a major military base and held my earliest memories. Like many military families, we lived in a large bungalow in the cantonment, where my father's regiment, the 14th Royal Indian Artillery, was based. He had given up teaching in 1942 to take up a wartime emergency commission and had rapidly reached the rank of Major because of his leadership and organisational ability and his familiarity with physics and mathematics—which were of immense use in the artillery in calculating ranges and trajectories. Though he had not been in active service against the Japanese during the World War II, he had spent a lot of time in Burma and Malaya as part of the contingent of troops helping to reassert British rule after three years' of occupation, mopping up and clearing out the remaining pockets of Japanese resistance.

I can still picture the bungalow, which was a classic white *chunam*[1] covered building with a portico, dating from the turn of the century. It was guarded by Sikh soldiers, who indulged me by taking me to their mess, propping me on the bar, and feeding me *ladoos* (a type of Indian sweet) much to the alarm of the ayah in whose charge I was. They also once frightened the life out of me when they saw an intruder in the fields around the house and pointed their rifles at him and clicked their rifle bolts as if to shoot. I can also remember my father coming back from a trip to Delhi bearing an electric kettle and, of all things, a bottle of Heinz peanut butter, both of which were novelties in those days.

We left Jhansi to stay with a family friend, a Mr Maud, an Englishman who had been an important District Collector in the Sunderbans in the dying days of the Raj but was now retired. This was a temporary base while my parents looked for permanent work. My mother,

---

[1] Chunam is a mixture of ground sea shells and lime, used to whitewash buildings

Marjorie, managed to get herself a short-term job locally teaching in St Hilda's School, where I was taken every day in the school bus and put into the kindergarten as a form of child-minding. I usually escaped and found my way to my mother's class and sat on the step outside the door waiting for her. My brother Wensley was sent to Breeks Memorial School, up on a hill in the centre of town, and my unemployed father looked after the infant John.

My father, Eric, had moved from north to south India. He was born in Lahore, one of the sons of Horace Thorpe, an Englishman who had left the British army to become a guard on the N W Railway and had no intention of returning to England—he felt he had nothing to return to as he had left England in the first place to avoid having to live with a stepfather. He had sent his sons to the Lawrence Royal Military School in Sanawar. My father had gone on to train as a teacher in the Lawrence College, Ghoragali and then got his first job in Bishop Cotton's School, Bangalore. In Bangalore he met my mother, Marjorie, the eldest daughter of parents from a railway family, they married and my brother, Wensley, was born in 1941. My parents then moved to the Lawrence School in Lovedale in the Nilgiri Hills, primarily because the school offered accommodation for married teachers. This job did not last too long as my father joined the army in 1942.

After Dad joined the army he was away on a number of postings—one of them unexpectedly extended when he was hospitalised in Malaya after suffering a severe reaction to the new drug penicillin. His regiment was part of the 33 Indian Corps commanded by Lieut. General Sir Montagu Stopford, and between April 1944 and May 1945 the Corps travelled over a thousand miles from Jorhat to Rangoon liberating 55,500 square miles of Japanese occupied India and Burma. The 33 Indian Corps also halted the northernmost Japanese drive into India at Kohima. In the course of the campaign they killed 23,600 Japanese and took about 1000 prisoner, and captured or destroyed 372 field guns.

On Dad's return, presumably on leave, I was conceived and born in Bangalore in 1946. It was decided to name me after my father's brother, Owen, who had been a Lieutenant in the 3/17 Dogra Regiment serving in Malaya and had been killed in the fall of Singapore—the family only found out that he had been killed when the war was over. He was murdered by a Japanese officer on the day of the British surrender of Singapore on 15 February 1942, when the troops were disarmed and he was waiting with a group of other officers from his regiment for the instrument of surrender to be signed at the Ford car factory. The Japanese officer had tossed a hand grenade into the group and we can only suppose that it was in revenge as Owen's regiment had opposed the first Japanese landings at Kota Baru, North Malaya, and inflicted very severe casualties on the invaders. In 2003 I found and visited Owen's grave in Kranji Cemetery, Singapore.

In between Bangalore and my father's posting to Jhansi, I missed India's Independence in August 1947 (well, to be fair I was only 17 months old and had other things to occupy my tiny mind) and missed Prime Minister Nehru's great 'Midnight Hour' speech delivered in the cultivated tones of a public school education at Harrow School and Cambridge University:

> 'At the stroke of the midnight hour, when the world sleeps, India will awake to life and freedom. A moment comes, which comes but rarely in history, when we step out from the old to the new, when an age ends, and when the soul of a nation, long suppressed, finds utterance.'

It sounded the starting gun for the great Anglo-Indian exodus.

Nehru's "when the world sleeps" was a piece of poetic licence. It would have been evening in Britain and Europe and the Americans and Canadians would have been contemplating their lunch.

Shortly before we left Jhansi, my younger brother,

John, had been born. My parents were convinced that after two boys the laws of chance dictated that they would have a girl and they decided to name the child Evelyn, after a friend who was a nurse in the hospital. Despite the arrival of yet another boy, they stuck with the name and my new brother was christened Evelyn John Thorpe—a first name he never used. My father justified his name on the grounds that Evelyn was a perfectly acceptable boy's name—citing as an example Evelyn Waugh, the author. But the name never stuck and he was always known as John. When later in life he went into the Royal Navy he never ever revealed what his first initial stood for—he daren't. He ended up formally changing his name to John by affidavit. It is interesting that if you take the first initial of the names of us brothers and sister in turn—Wensley, Owen, Evelyn and Susan, you get WOES—which is what, I suspect, our parents sometimes thought of us.

Our stay in Ooty did not last long and we left in June 1950 for Coimbatore, down on the plains, where my parents had secured jobs in Stanes High School—my father as Assistant Headmaster, my mother as a teacher. Coimbatore was an important cotton textile town, the 'Manchester of South India', and also was a big centre for engineering and peanut growing. It was the gateway to the Nilgiri Hills and Ooty, Lovedale and Conoor where people went to escape the heat of the summer—even though Coimbatore itself had a reasonably pleasant climate. It had a big railway junction and even an airport to accommodate the one Indian Airlines Dakota, ex-World War II, which flew in each day. As the sight of aircraft was a novelty, all play in the school playgrounds would stop whenever the daily plane flew over.

Stanes High School (Motto: Aim for the Highest) was founded in 1862 by Robert Stanes, a philanthropic coffee and tea planter. His business became a thriving tea and coffee company, T. Stanes and Co., which produced the first instant coffee in India in the 1950s and our family were one of the first people to test sample it—it came in an unappetising brown and yellow striped tin and the contents tasted strange to our family who had been brought up on freshly ground Mysore or Malabar coffee. We didn't think it would catch on! Stanes School was a co-educational boarding cum day school and the pupils were a mixture of Anglo-Indians, many from railway families in the remoter parts where schooling was a problem—some on free scholarships as they were from poor families, and the richer Indians, mainly the children of well-to-do textile and engineering factory owners and peanut growers, who paid fees. It stood on a large site on one of the main roads, and had several commanding buildings—the main school block had an impressive classical portico. It was bordered on all sides by extensive playing fields.

After a few days living with the Headmaster while our accommodation was being got ready, we moved to a bungalow on the boundary of the main cricket field, at the other end of which was the much grander two-storied Headmaster's house that we had just left. Having a bungalow to ourselves was in recognition of my father's status as Assistant Headmaster—all the other teachers who lived in school had to make do with rooms in the dormitory buildings. Our bungalow, which was typical of those constructed in the early 1900s, consisted of a sitting room, dining room and a large bedroom—all interconnected. Behind these ran two rudimentary bathrooms which basically had a cold tap and an outlet for the water—the original 'wet rooms' now so beloved of the exponents of fashionable living. There was a covered veranda and storeroom. A kitchen and godown[1] were attached, almost as afterthoughts. The cooking oven was fashioned, as was traditional, from baked earth with a dressing of cow-dung over it, which was supposed to have antiseptic properties. This dressing, collected fresh from the fields by our servants, was diluted with water and regularly re-applied. My parents drew the line at al-

---

1   a storage shed, but it was used as servants' quarters.

lowing the servants to use pats of dried cow-dung as fuel largely, I suppose, because the drying process would involve the cook splatting the pats against the nearest convenient house wall to dry in the sun.

To provide more space, half the verandah that ran round the front of the house had been enclosed with plywood to create an L-shaped extra bedroom in which my brothers and I slept. As the windows in this 'room' looked out on the cricket ground, we had a wonderful grandstand view of the games. There was a large and shady neem tree at the side, which was to prove an entertaining plaything, doubling as a fort or a ship and whose branches would in time support home-made swings.

Plumbing in the house was rudimentary and we relied on 'thunder boxes' as flush toilets had yet to come our way. The 'sweeper', whose duty it was to keep the toilets clean, hovered outside and came in promptly to empty the 'potties' after use! Luckily he once spotted a small snake that had crept in and coiled itself around the leg of one of the thunder boxes—being nipped by the asp when one was in a most vulnerable position would not have been good! Water for bathing or washing was stored in an old oil drum. Baths were, naturally, cold, but not a problem in the tropical climate.

Our drinking water was always boiled, strained through muslin cloth and then kept cool in an earthenware *'goglet'* fitted with a brass tap. The evaporation of the water seeping through the slightly porous earthenware provided the cooling effect. Of course there was no refrigeration, we relied on meatsafes—wooden cabinets with wire mesh sides and fronts to ensure a draught flowed through and kept the food cool. The legs of these cabinets stood in stone dishes of water to prevent the ever present ants getting at the contents. As most of our food was bought fresh every day from market, there was really nothing much to spoil in the heat.

Our family was looked after by our team of servants, who consisted of a female cook, an ayah (maid) and the sweeper. There was also a *mali*, or gardener, who visited each evening to look after the front garden and worked valiantly to keep the plants alive in the heat by watering them with water carried in a goatskin. The servants were paid a pittance, but got their food and accommodation. They came and went at my mother's whim. Only very occasionally would they have children who lodged with them in their godown; these children became instant companions and probably improved my Tamil no end as they did not speak a word of English.

At the back of the house, just outside the school's boundary fence was a large and very deep well. The well's opening covered a huge area, about that of two tennis courts, and there was a path that wound down through the dense vegetation growing on the rocky sides until it reached the water's edge. The water was clear and dark and was of swimming pool proportions. This was not a well where one could sling a bucket over the side; drawing water involved a lengthy and dangerous walk down the slippery path, so no one chanced it. Instead, the school had run a pipeline to the water and pumped it up into storage tanks near our house. Our family probably drank and bathed in the stuff. One hot summer, Wensley, having recently learned to swim, decided to try to cool off in the well. Having negotiated the tricky path, he dived in only to be shocked rigid by the freezing water. He was in difficulty and my father had to rush down and haul him out before he drowned.

There was a mystery about this house that I was never able to solve. At the side of it, in a scrubby area where nobody but us boys ever went, was a grove of overgrown yellow oleander trees. The curious thing about them was that they were hung with small, bloodstained parcels of gunny (hessian) sacking—which struck me as being very sinister and we were too scared to see what was in them. Our servants would never go anywhere near this area. I've mentioned this to people recently who tell me that these parcels contained afterbirths and were placed there to thank the gods for the successful delivery of children—but there may be another explanation. I've never come across this anywhere else.

The house was kept cool by ceiling-mounted electric fans which creaked their way through the hot afternoons and nights. Thinly slatted bamboo 'chicks' and fragrant khus khus[1] panels hung over the doors and windows to keep out the hot breezes. The effect of the fans was somewhat limited at night as the use of mosquito nets was a must. Creepy crawlies were common. Indoors we had the common house lizards, known as 'flycatchers', and a variety of spiders—they were tolerated because they ate the other insects. The lizards had a disconcerting habit of losing their grip on the ceiling, possibly because they encountered a powdery patch of the white-wash used to paint the rooms, and would fall off and scurry away, frightening the occupants of the room. We would sometimes grab them by their tails, which they would break off in order to escape—apparently the tails grew back again. I once saw a lizard fall down the back of a large female relative with explosive results—and possibly the fastest strip-tease in history, certainly the loudest! Outside we encountered flies, ants, spiders and beetles of many sorts. I developed a special horror of the very large stag beetles that flew around after the monsoon rains in June and July, we called them *bundoos* in South

---

1   Khus khus screens are made from the aromatic fibrous root of Indian grass *vetivera zizanioides*

India. And I hated the clouds of flying ants and moths that crowded the lights at night during the rainy season if a door or mesh screen had been accidentally left open. The servants would hang sprigs of aromatic plants around the outside lights to deter the insects—as I recall, these were less than useless.

Anyone who has lived in India will know the drama that is the monsoon. Those still, humid, sticky June days that precede it becoming increasingly sultry and close as the cloud cover grows. The family becoming irritable and listless and it was difficult to sleep at night, which added to our bad tempers. Then a gentle breeze would slowly pick up, sending the dust spiralling off the ground and into the house, stinging our eyes and coating the lovingly polished teak or rosewood furniture—polished by the servants, I might add, not by us—nobody in the family did any housework. The breeze would give way to a sudden stillness, the temperature would plummet and the sky would darken as "on a thundering chariot of clouds"[1] the monsoon came. The clouds, black with rain from the Arabian Sea, boiled and massed overhead, turning day into twilight, the gloom suddenly split by spectacular crackling lightning and booming bursts of thunder—fol-

---

[1] 'In the rainy gloom of July nights on a thundering chariot of clouds he comes, comes, ever comes.' From Rabindranath Tagore's poem Gitanjali

lowed by the first sprinkling of rain. We would be off with our shirts and shoes and out into the open, squealing with excitement, looking up at the sky and eagerly anticipating the main event.

It would become quite dark and threatening and the sprinkle of rain would suddenly increase in force as if a hand had reached out and turned on a Heavenly tap. The sky would explode with a deluge slashing, hissing and drumming along roofs and streets, the force of the raindrops stinging our faces and backs—hard and cold. Each drop striking the ground in a puff of dust and, as the thirsty earth was quenched, you could smell the hot, steamy dust, which rose briefly in a brown vapour. Then, as the rain hammered down, it brought with it the unfamiliar sound of rivulets and torrents as the water ran off roofs and trees and streamed along the ground. The noise was quite something—hissing rain, thunder and lightning, the sounds of rushing water, the drumming on corrugated tin roofs—and the excited shouts of children, adults too, dancing in the deluge, splashing in unaccustomed puddles, the screams and cries competing with the wild cawing of crows and other birds flying round in celebration. When the rain stopped, the evenings would be made soft by the cool wet breeze, the scents of flowers and damp earth, the chirping of crickets and a sky washed bright, glittering with stars. And of course those bloody flying ants.

By and by, as the monsoon days progressed, the novelty wore off and we came to detest the incessant, inconvenient downpours. Being used to wandering around lightly clad and lightly encumbered, we did not like having to wear raincoats, which were very warm and clammy, or carry umbrellas—and of course it meant that break times were spent sheltering in the school corridors and the evening games of football or hockey became messy and muddy—or were called off altogether because the pitches were too wet and soggy. The insects which emerged in their thousands with the rain and got into the houses were an added irritation.

I love the spectacle of thunder and lightning and used to stand out in the rains to see the show. My parents thought I was eccentric and my father, who loved a joke, once dared me to stand out in the open, shake my fist at the sky and shout, 'I defy you to strike me.' I did and, predictably, this was followed by the spectacular crack of a lightning bolt. Far from frightening me, I would do it secretly to see if I could get it to happen again. My wife, unfortunately, has a phobia about lightning and thunder because her mother used to get under a table with the children whenever there was a storm—I can only presume that her mother's mother in turn did the same. I loved standing out in the pouring rain, which in India cooled the heat of the day but yet was warm enough to be comforting; no one worried about you getting your clothes soaking wet. I sailed paper boats, with ants as passengers, and raced them against twigs and bottle tops in the streams of water that suddenly sprang up. That unforgettable smell of the first rain on warm ground still brings back the memories.

The monsoon rains are crucial to the farmers of India. A bad monsoon means a bad harvest or even drought, which could have a devastating effect on the economy and on the well-being of families. If the monsoon fails, there could be famine. Though the building of dams and irrigation canals is helping to avoid the worst effects of a poor monsoon, as recently as 2002 there was a drought in Gujarat when the rains failed. The Indian Government takes the monsoon seriously and monitors its progress through the India Meteorological Department. Predicting the monsoon though has proved to be difficult as accurate and reliable forecasts are not easy to make. It is thought that the monsoon is very dependent on sea and air temperatures but, despite all of the expert observations and statistics, and the power of modern computers, it is proving hard to get it right every time. The first place in India to see the monsoon is Thiruvananthapuram—which used to be called Trivandrum—and the local Met Department's predictions on when they will receive the first monsoon rains are headline national news.

3
Off To School

I was enrolled in the junior Kindergarten but, because I was already a voracious reader, was judged to be advanced enough to skip a class and go ahead a year—then called a 'double promotion'. Progression from year to year in school was dependent on passing the final examination each December and I remember being in some classes with poor unfortunates who had failed to get promoted for a couple of years and were therefore considerably older than the rest of us. One of them, Dan, had failed the Fourth Standard twice—and failed it again when I was there. Dan, I hope you've got out by now!

We wore a uniform of khaki shorts and shirts, black shoes and white socks. Our shorts were held up by canvas belts in the school colours, with an 'S shaped' snake forming the buckle. The girls wore royal blue gymslips. This uniform was fairly common across Anglo-Indian schools in India and I encountered it again and again in my six changes of school. I was given a khaki solar topi—a pith helmet—to ward off the sun, but it was never worn and was eventually reduced to duty as an impromptu football.

My teacher, a Miss Pharoah, was sweet, plump and encouraging and I got on well at school. She didn't turn up one day and after a lot of whispering among the teachers, we were finally told at assembly that she had unexpectedly died—she must have been in her thirties at most. She had, apparently, had a heart attack. We children were too young to really grasp the significance of death, but we did miss our lovely, smiling Mrs Pharoah. Her replacement turned out to be no less accommodating and we soon settled down again—but I did wonder how someone's heart could simply stop, just like that! The adults didn't want to talk about it

Indian schools were strict on discipline. Minor misdemeanours brought detention or 'a hundred lines'. Corporal punishment was routine: 'cuts' on the palm, or the knuckles, with a ruler from the teacher and, for more serious offences, the trip to the Headmaster's office for 'six of the best' with the cane, again on the hands.

It was also not unusual for some teachers to throw the wooden-backed blackboard duster at the heads of pupils who were misbehaving or to lay about them with a ruler. Misdemeanours committed at PT or games could result in quite strenuous physical punishment such as being made to run round the field in the heat, or do push-ups till your arms collapsed. We children accepted all of this as a fact of life and our parents, far from complaining, expected iron discipline—and good results.

I made two visits to the Headmaster's office in my years there when, later, my father was acting Headmaster—and received an extra beating at home on each occasion. The first time was bizarre. Another teacher's son had been caught vandalising the toilets and in the interrogation that followed tried to spin a yarn that would implicate others and so mitigate his own offence. For some reason, the others included me, and we found ourselves accused of 'doing wicked things' in the toilets. As we hadn't done anything we denied it of course, but in the perverted logic of schoolmasters we were bound to deny it, weren't we, while they had a co-offender who had already confessed. So, all of us got caned. The second time was when the same boy found a way into the kindergarten room during the school holidays, via a loose window, pilfered some toys which he shared with me as I played with him and his brother—we were the only kids left in school as our parents lived there. I was 'caught in possession' and the three of us were caned.

Almost as bad as the caning was the humiliating ritual that accompanied it. A messenger arrived at your classroom door and asked you to report to the Head. You then waited shiftily and in a state of terror outside the Headmaster's office, under the scrutiny of all passers by, who knew what was about to happen and regarded you with thinly veiled amusement. Then, the trip back to class after the caning, hands stinging, trying not to cry, red faced and shaking with the adrenaline rush, while your classmates regarded you silently, some smugly—the bastards. During break time, your hands were closely examined by your curious classmates, wincing at the 'cuts' across your palms. Having calmed down by then, your bragging instincts took over and you exaggerated your version of events to impress your friends with your bravery.

Life as a schoolboy in 1950's India was full of simple, straightforward and mostly inexpensive pleasures as we had to make do with what was around. The playground games were seasonal. We played marbles with ones made of glass and clay, the best were steel ball bearings, known as 'dormies', which we got from boys whose fathers worked on the railway. We played *gilly dandoo*[1], and were lucky not to be seriously injured by the *gilly* flying at some speed when it was well struck by the *dandoo* and we were trying to catch it! Some years later I managed to loosen John's front teeth with a well struck *gilly*—fortunately they seemed to recover. We played with spinning tops which we customised with a sharpened spike designed to damage the opponent's top. The spike was usually made from a steel screw with the screwdriving end sharpened to a point by rubbing it on a piece of stone, or sometimes shaping it like a chisel so it could take a chip off the opponent's top; if you were very skilful and very lucky, you could split it in two. The poshest tops were made of expensive rosewood, which was supposed to be tougher. Spin was imparted by winding a cord, which we called a *jhartie*, round the top, then bringing your arm down with considerable force as though whipping. It was almost compulsory to lick the end of the string when applying it to the top to give it better adhesion. This must have had good bacterial qualities and hugely stimulated our immune systems. The other end of the *jhartie* was held in place against your fingers by

---

[1] 'gully danda in N. India, 'tip cat' in the West—you struck a small banana-shaped piece of wood (the gilly or gully) with a foot long wooden baton (dandoo or danda) to hit it as far a possible. The game is of course more complicated than that.

threading it through a soda water bottle cap with a hole punched through it.

We played a variety of ball games, such as 'horly korly', where the object was basically to hit one another as stingingly as possible with a tennis or rubber ball, and 'seven tiles', where one team tried to construct a tower of seven pieces of tile or stone while the other tried to hit them with the ball—which rendered them 'out'.

Spring brought the kite season. We flew home-made tissue paper kites, the very manoeuvrable tail-less Indian fighting kites, with strings made lethal with pasted on ground glass, known as *manja*. We scoured the house for old light bulbs, ground them to powder, mixed this with flour paste and colour from the bazaar—and applied the lot carefully to our kite string, which was stretched round a couple of trees. The *manja* was necessary in order to entangle and cut the kites of opponents and its constant use left deep cuts in your index finger and thumb. The skill at kite flying was amazing and the best flyers could manoeuvre to cut an opponent's kite string with just a finely judged tug, manage to wrap it round their own and bring both kites to earth. More often than not, a cut kite simply drifted away, followed by a procession of chasing small boys anxious to get hold of it when it came to earth. In the melee that followed the kite was often destroyed—and quite a few small boys got damaged too when, with eyes fixed firmly on a drifting kite, they collided with walls and trees or fell into ditches.

There was a periodic fashion for collecting beetles called 'gold bees' which were brown, thumb-sized insects with an iridescent green collar, and the smaller 'guava bees' which were iridescent green all over. We carried them around in shoeboxes filled with a bedding of sand to encourage them to lay eggs—which they did—and they were sometimes traded for cash. We rode the dhobis' (washer men's) donkeys, which would go from placid to vicious in an instant and the experience was like riding a very noisy and bad tempered bucking bronco. They accounted for a few fractured arms and broken collar bones. Some of the more foolhardy boys tried to enliven the experience by attempting to tie tin cans filled with pebbles to the donkeys' tails, but I never saw anyone succeed as a kick from the hind legs was sufficient deterrent. We discovered that we could torment the crows by kicking around a piece of black tissue paper, which they thought was an injured crow, prompting them to dive bomb and attack us in an effort to save their companion. I'm afraid that we thought this was hilarious.

Hunting was a favourite sport, conducted with home made catapults, known colloquially as the 'cattie', some of them quite lethal as their rubbers were cut from the very strong vacuum rubber used on steam trains—again provided by boys who came from railway families[1]. During the weekends, boys roamed the school grounds with their catties killing anything that ran, crawled or flew. Of special interest were the large chameleons known to us as 'buffies' which we streamed after like a hunting pack, chasing them from tree to tree, firing stones until we brought them down. Few got away. My brother Wensley was clever with his hands and fashioned very good catapults and kites. I once saw him hit a brilliantly feathered blue-green hoopoe at about fifty yards—Wensley still has regrets about killing it as he thought he stood no chance of hitting it. Many of us ran around barefoot, heedless of the thorns or stony ground, just like the local chokras, or shod in our Bata 'keds'—thin canvas plimsolls with a working life of about three months before your toes began to come through the canvas. The keds were obtainable only in white or a horrible shade of rusty brown.

And then there were the native chokras. Sometimes we would turn our attentions to hunting them, pelting them with stones and abusing their parentage in fluent Tamil—and they gave back as good as they got. It was tribal, and was expected—rather like a formal diplomatic greeting. Either side would have been astonished, and upset, if ritual abuse followed by volleys of stones

---

1   the railways were also a source of gauge glass tubes for pea shooters.

did not take place. At other times, hostilities would be set aside and we would play together in the sandpits in the park, challenging each other to games of *kabaddi*[1] or *gilly dandoo*.

The chokras didn't seem to mind what you called them as long as you didn't use the word 'bloody'—then they went wild because they did not understand its meaning but regarded it as being very bad indeed! When Indians got really mad at you, you could wind them up by saying, 'Don't show red eyes to me', don't ask me why. It was the same with Sikhs, for whom the ultimate insult was to ask whether it had gone 12 o'clock (noon)! I have no idea of the origin of the insult but it was apparently to do with suggesting their brains were boiling in their turbans in the noonday sun. Of course there were cruder, sometimes quite creative (and physically impossible) terms of abuse. I've forgotten a lot of my Tamil, but not the 'bad words'.

I was a keen participant in the regular team games, football, cricket and hockey, and played after school

---

1 In kabaddi two teams face each other on a badminton court-sized pitch. Members of each team advance into the other's territory repeatedly saying 'kabbadi' and not drawing breath. The object is to touch a member of the opposing team and escape back into your own territory, rendering them 'out'. The other team tries to grab the intruder and pin him down until he draws breath, when he is then declared 'out'.

hours for my house team. It was common to split teams into 'skins' and 'shirts'. The 'skins' played topless—it's a pity that this didn't spread to the girls' school. Athletics was also very popular. Wensley was enrolled one summer holiday in an athletics coaching scheme and used to come home every evening and tell me what he had learned. It certainly improved my high jump technique as I progressed to the Western Roll and the Straddle, leaping over a rope strung between two chairs in our bedroom falling onto our mattresses laid on the concrete floor. Of course those styles of jumping have been overtaken by the Fosbury Flop—which relies on a pumped up airbed of a pit to break your fall—our thin cotton mattresses would have broken our necks. Despite the surrogate coaching I was never very good at athletics. My worst sport was the cricket ball throw event where distance counted. However, all that throwing had a lasting effect as I am now pretty deadly at the coconut shy. It's not length, it's what you do with it that counts, eh?

The British public school 'House' system operated as it did in most Anglo-Indian schools. We had three Houses, Lions, Tigers and Panthers—I found myself in Tigers House. Cross country was a favourite sport of mine and an opportunity for the whole school to race together, starting early in the morning and lining up outside the school railings. Despite my indifferent performances in athletics, I prospered in the cross country and generally did well—often in the top twenty or thirty in the school (I was only eight or nine years old). I was a tolerable hockey player and cricketer. I tended to be the wicketkeeper in the scratch cricket games we sometimes played among friends, mainly because I had makeshift wicket-keeper's gloves—they were fox fur gloves that belonged to my mother and were part of an ensemble that included a no longer fashionable fur jacket—for which there was absolutely no call in the tropical heat.

Early on, when I was in the Kindergarten, aged about five, I was down to take part in the usual children's 50 yard dash on sports day, where every child got sweets at the finish line. For some reason, possibly aping the bigger boys training seriously for the school sports, I took this equally seriously and practised for weeks before sports day. My mother, amused, added to the joke by having a pair of white satin running shorts made, complete with yellow and black stripes down the sides—the colours of Tigers' House. These were well used in my sweaty practice runs and on the great day the shorts were washed and hung out to dry ready for use that afternoon. Disaster struck! The local baker, Mr Morritt, had a pet deer who roamed the school grounds; it took a fancy to my shorts and ate them off the washing line. I was inconsolable. Mrs Morritt offered compensation in the form of cakes, but to no avail. I had to wear ordinary shorts for the event and I maintain, to this day, that this affected my performance.

Revenge was mine, however, when shortly afterwards the deer got bitten by a snake and died. The Morritts had it skinned and very kindly made me a pair of deerskin shoes. It was tempting to put them on and kick the crap out of them in revenge. But I was too proud of my brown suede deerskins to do so.

The big athletics meeting of the year was the annual Quadrangular Sports, in which four schools, Stanes, Montfort School from Yercaud, and Vestry and Campion schools from Trichinopoly[1] competed and took it in turn to host. The competition was intense and we became familiar with the best of the athletes—Kenny Bosen from our school, who went on to become All-India javelin champion, and the Lavender brothers from Vestry who specialised in the shot-put and discus. Montfort had an unfair advantage as they had a number of Iraqi boys who had been sent over to study English; they were much bigger, older and stronger than the rest and dominated some track events, and were particularly good at boxing as the big ones were too large and powerful, and the small ones were extremely aggressive.

---

[1] Now known as Thiruchirapalli—try saying that when you've had a few!

I occasionally used to 'fetch' for Kenny Bosen when he practiced the javelin in the school fields in the evenings—running it back to him at the end of each throw. His brother, Derek, was the school's hockey goalie—an excellent one and fearless—with only a pair of pads on his legs for protection unlike the zombie-looking 'goal minders' of today. As we played on baked earth *'mutti'* hockey-pitches, hockey was a dangerous game. Apart from the hazards of getting clouted by a stick or a hard-hit ball, you risked serious gravel burns if you fell over. Wensley was very friendly with the Bosens, whose father was in the Police, they lived in the Police Lines near the school. One kite season they made a giant kite, out of newspaper, I think, and stuck it together with paste made from flour. It just about got off the ground and was not one of the great successes in the annals of flight. My father also used to go over and Mr Bosen and he would use the police firing range to amuse themselves firing old Martini-Henry rifles dating from the late 1800s.

4
Feeding And Entertaining The Inner And Outer Chokra

Our day began with one or other of us children having to get up and make my parents' morning coffee. This wasn't a chore as, unknown to my parents, a perk of the job was to gobble spoonfuls of the powdered milk that we used. We ate four square meals a day. Breakfast was porridge, which could be oats, *suji* (semolina) or *ragi*—which was toasted millet flour which looks and tastes a bit like chocolate—followed by eggs, toast and coffee. Lunch was curry and rice and fruit or a couple of boiled sweets, always a couple, never more, for dessert. To confuse my young brother John we used to call them TLWs, until he twigged. Tea was taken at about 4 o'clock and was bread, tinned Kraft cheese and tinned IXL jam[1] and cakes—we were particularly fond of the Japanese Cakes we got from a Swiss baker, these were a sandwich of two almond macaroons with cream in the middle and a chocolate drop on top. We washed all of this down with pots of Nilgiri tea.

Dinner, inevitably at 8 o'clock, was of three courses—soup, main dish and pudding. I still eat mine at 8. We dined on all the special Anglo-Indian dishes: vindaloo, *panthras* (rolled pancakes with a mince filling, coated with breadcrumbs and fried), *jhal frazie*, country captain and, the all time favourite potato cutlets also known as *aloo chops*. When I came to England, I was disappointed to find that the famous English fish and chips were bland and soggy, unlike the crisp and spicy masala fried fish we were used to.

We also took full advantage of the free fruit around us growing in the school grounds and in the park next door. We stripped tamarind trees (the tamarind pods which are yellowy green just before they ripen were a favou-

---

[1] imported Australian jam, whose name was misappropriated in later years by the rock band INXS.

rite), guava trees and mango trees. In the hills we ate passion fruit and loquats off the bushes, and of course raided the pear orchards. More desperately, we tried to manufacture chewing gum from the sap of the oleander trees, and ate the petals, especially the speckled white ones, off the 'Mayflower' trees—whose proper name was the Gul Mohur. I also remember eating star apples from the trees in Calcutta, trying to eat the red berries off the banyan trees—which are a type of fig—and eating a plum known as a *'jumblum'* in Madras but a *'kala jamoon'* in Calcutta, which was a particular favourite of the flying foxes who occasionally electrocuted themselves on the power wires running above the tree.

During school break times, we would flock to the boundary wall to buy stuff off the vendors who gathered there. The ice cream wallah dispensed 'ice fruits' (ice lollies) from his tricycle-mounted icebox. Other vendors sold slices of cucumber sprinkled with chilli powder and salt, or peanuts and sticky toffee balls made of puffed rice and caramel or caramel and gram biscuits—known as *'jow muttais'* as they stretched like tough meat. The quantities of peanuts and puffed rice were measured out in specially designed metal cans—the common measures were seers, chittacks and ollocks! I also loved eating *'noongoos'*—palm fruits, like transparent jelly (known also as *'thalsas'*) which the man brought in a large earthenware jar filled with ice chippings. We were not great fans of the school tuck shop with its boring sweets and biscuits and largely because we wanted quantity, the pockets of our shorts filled to bursting with peanuts, like swollen cows' udders. The only things I bought from the tuck shop were sticks of Egyptian brand chewing gum, which were unobtainable elsewhere.

Despite the enormous quantities of food, we remained stick-thin because of the heat and our own perpetual motion as we walked or ran everywhere. It is only in later life that this bad diet has come back to haunt us people from South Asia with the high incidence of diabetes, high blood pressure, stroke and heart disease.

Our clothes were custom made, nearly everyone's were. Every so often, and especially at Christmas and Easter, we visited the cloth cum tailor shop in the market, chose the material and were measured for shirts and shorts. The colours never seemed to vary, white or buff. Though it was possible to buy shoes from Bata's shop—their 'naughty boy's' shoes for schoolboys—it was cheaper to have the cobbler come to our house at regular intervals (how did he know our shoes needed replacing?). He traced the outlines of growing feet on a sheet of newspaper and produced the black school shoes to a standard pattern a few weeks later complete with steel Blakey studs hammered into the soles and heels to extend their life. The hawker visited regularly with his carefully arranged pack full of buttons, ribbons and lace; it was amazing the variety and amount of stuff he could cram into his pack, which was carried over his shoulder. The barber called to give us haircuts; we sat on the verandah in a dining chair and he gave us a basic buzz cut, which we called the 'soup bowl.'

Every morning the milkman called with his brass pails of well watered-down milk. There were coils of straw in the pails to prevent the milk from slopping, and the milk had to be boiled to ensure it was safe to drink. We would skim off the cream and eat it with sugar. I am sure that any Anglo-Indian who lived in India or Pakistan will be able to recall the wonderful smell of milk that has accidentally boiled over—it was a devil to get off the saucepan, but of course we weren't doing the getting off! Some families relied on condensed milk as they could not trust the local supply—my Grandmother, who lived in Bangalore, used it liberally and later got me addicted to condensed milk in my morning coffee. A very special treat was the first milk when a cow had calved. It was extra thick and was sort of fried and eaten with sugar—it looked like scrambled eggs.

On Sundays we would be visited by the *iddly* man who sold us *iddlies* and *sambar* (steamed rice cakes and curry) and hoppers (sweet, frilly coconut milk pancakes) for our breakfast. The cook made the daily trip to the market for meat and vegetables—because, remember, everything had to be bought fresh. Breakfast, when all the family was together, was the occasion for the familiar mantra, 'What do you want for lunch and dinner?', so that the cook could be given her orders for the day before she went to market.

My short, 'soup-bowl' haircut was plastered down with liberal lashings of coconut oil, very popular in South India and believed to strengthen the hair! It also attracted the ants and I awoke several times with an itchy scalp to find my hair and pillow covered with small black ants that had come to feast on the coconut oil. After that I switched to Brylcreem, which the ants didn't find attractive, nor did I.

Nothing was wasted and it was far less of a throw-away society than it is now. We collected our newspapers and bottles and sold them periodically to the roving *bikriwallahs*—an efficient and profitable form of recycling. Any zinc bathtubs that developed leaks were fixed with solder by itinerant tinkers, mackintoshes that needed waterproofing were treated in some sort of petrol/kerosene mixture by roaming waterproofers, and pillows and mattresses were fluffed up by cotton beaters who appeared once a year with something that looked like a large archery bow and fluffed the cotton by twanging the string through it. We were taught how to sew on buttons—the zip fly was yet to come our way—and were expected to make our own running repairs when fly buttons fell off. Of course we put this off until we were almost in danger of indecent exposure. Naturally our clothes were handed down from brother to brother.

On the entertainment front, Radio was very limited as most of the programmes were in Tamil or Hindi, with programmes in English only at certain times. My father religiously listened to the BBC World Service news each night on a valve-driven Bush radio that had to warm up before it played—it had a 'magic eye' that glowed green to ensure you were properly tuned to the station. For pop music, I was hooked on Radio Ceylon, especially the weekly Binaca Hit Parade (which was sponsored by the makers of Binaca toothpaste). In due course my father acquired a second hand Decca gramophone from the local priest, Canon Caldicott. This was the newer model with a 'ceramic' cartridge, as opposed to the older gramophones with steel needles. He played the same four or five classical 'long playing' records that came with it over and over again while pretending to conduct the orchestra. Come to think of it, as it was impossible to obtain 'long playing' records in Coimbatore, Canon Caldicott probably got fed up with the ones he owned so sold the whole system on to a new audience.

Caldicott was a periodic visitor to our house to play chess and drink whisky with my father—and in doing so probably suffered having to listen to his records again. He was a Churchillian figure of a man whose fingers had been chopped off at the first joint by the Japanese when they had tortured him. Very much Low Church, he hated incense and ritual; he persuaded my father to be a lay preacher at Evensong, mainly so he, Caldicott, could get an occasional evening off, I think. To my father's credit, he gave better sermons than Caldicott ever did. I was a choirboy and therefore spent Sundays at church for both morning and evening services. A measure of our Low Church status was illustrated by the fact that the choir vestry and robing room did not have a religious picture but one of Winston Churchill—and his eyes did follow you around the room. When Caldicott went on holiday, his place was filled by a High Church priest who came, I think, from Keti in the hills. This priest loved incense, bells and sweeping his arms extravagantly round as though he was doing the butterfly stroke to bring his palms together in the praying position. We choirboys found this both fascinating and vastly amusing.

Saturdays, however, meant a much anticipated and regular trip to the cinema. We had two cinemas showing English language films, the Rainbow and the Shrinivas.

We would go early for the 3 o'clock or 6 o'clock shows, lining up to buy the cheapest tickets, which cost 6 annas (about 1/200th of a £), and which permitted you to sit in the front row of the cinema, closest to the screen on a cheap tin chair, and there was usually some money left over to afford a paper cone of peanuts or 'hot stuff'— variously known as 'hot gram' or '*dhal mote*', and now in England popular as Bombay Mix. The film was signalled in both cinemas by the playing of 'Tiger Rag' and 'Sixteen Tons', I don't know why—maybe they were records supplied by the film distributors. There were trailers, cartoons and the Indian News Review before the main film. We loved it. On Christmas Day 1955 our parents took us first to the photographer's studio (the photo of us children is in this book) and then to the cinema where, in the expensive balcony seats we sat on sofas and ate ice cream—it was good, but not as enjoyable.

Our other entertainment was when the European missionaries of the Society for Promoting Christian Knowledge (SPCK) made their annual visit to the school. We were spared lessons to attend their telling of Bible stories illustrated by Biblical figures made of felt cleverly placed on ingenious felt scenery which pulled back to reveal other scenes. The missionaries were friendly and introduced us to strange games—paddle tennis, which was played with tennis balls and huge ping pong bats, and something called crocker, which was cricket with soccer balls. The object of all of this was to sell bibles and holy pictures and to persuade Christian boys and girls to be 'saved'. It all seems horribly unethical in retrospect, but we enjoyed their visits and few if any conversions were made or pupils 'saved'—or if they were, the magic did not last for long. But these eccentric Englishmen were friendly in the way our teachers weren't and we delighted in their company and their genuine warmth.

The school also acquired its own permanent representative from the missionaries, a strange, thin, pale Englishman with round glasses, called Dr. Herman (not his real name, I've changed it in case he's still around)—but called by the boys *vellai poondoo* which means 'white garlic' in Tamil. Herman was said to be a qualified doctor, and was also the PE master. His quirk was to punish boys who misbehaved by calling them to his room, taking their trousers down and caning them on their bare bottoms—then giving them a glass of his home-made lemonade or ginger beer. He also encouraged the boys to visit his room to play games of table football and cricket and listen to his records of English comedians speaking in dialect—you can imagine the weird scene in the playground of boys with decidedly Anglo-Tamil accents trying to imitate a broad Yorkshire accent. In modern times, Dr. Herman's behaviour would probably qualify him for a stern visit from social services!

The travelling Shakespeare company came our way too—Shakespeareana, the troupe run by the actress Felicity Kendall's parents, Geoffrey Kendall and Laura Liddell. Their production of the Merchant of Venice was my introduction to Shakespeare. The troupe stayed at our house in later years and their travelling show was the subject of the Merchant-Ivory film, Shakespearewalla. I met Felicity's parents—I was turned out of my room to accommodate them when my father was Headmaster—and also met her sister, Jennifer and husband who was later the very popular Indian film actor, Shashi Kapoor.

My father was also successful in enticing the captain of the Indian test cricket team, the famous Polly Umrigar, to visit our school one day to give the boys cricket coaching in the nets. One of the boys managed to bowl him out and was a hero for the rest of the week. Umrigar died in November 2006, as I was writing this.

I took part regularly in the school's Speech Day concerts both as the recipient of prizes and because I was usually acting in one of the entertainments. I was also inevitably one of the Three Kings in the nativity play—I suspect because it amused my parents that I had to struggle for the high notes in the verse each King had to sing to explain the gift they had brought:

> "*Frankincense to offer have I,*
> *Incense owns a Deity nigh.*
> *Prayer and praising* [panic beginning to set in] *all men rrrraaaiiising* [strangled cry—audience giggles and laughter]
> *Worship Him God most High.*" [Red-faced with exertion and embarrassment, but relieved it is over and is now someone else's turn for the musical torture. Shove gift of 'Frankincense' at grinning Joseph]

My parents loved to tease me about it—they had a bizarre sense of what was humorous.

Next to the school was the very large Chidambaram Pillai[1] Park. My brothers and I used its swings and concrete slides, imagined we were cowboys as we rode the two stone Nandi bulls that flanked its gate, and roamed its grounds. We collected *goondamanis*, small red seeds from pods on the trees—these could also be bought in souvenir shops where they were hollowed out and filled with a half-dozen or so tiny ivory elephants. *Goondamanis* were excellent ammunition for pea shooters. We also teased a plant that grew by a stream; touching its leaves caused them to fold up sharply. I have since found out

---

[1] He was an Indian freedom fighter and lawyer.

that this is known as the 'sensitive plant', *mimosa pudica*, and the leaves fold when touched because of changes in water pressure at the base of the leaflets, triggered by electrical impulses that run through the plant. Amazing. And amazing too how little it took to keep us amused.

The park also hosted regular high-volume political meetings, the occasional Coimbatore 'Olympics', marathon cycling endurance tests that ran for days and nights and an annual 'Exhibition' of industrial goods and novelty items. This exhibition was on for about a month and we would eventually be allowed a day there where we wandered around the elaborate pavilions devoted to agricultural innovations, textiles or new machinery—but our interest was in the fairground rides and the exotic (for us) snacks like popcorn and candy floss. As is the Indian way, the exhibition serenaded us from midday to midnight with film songs and excitedly hysterical announcements from its high-volume loudspeakers. This was in competition with the regular serenade of devotional and South Indian classical music pumped out from the loudspeakers attached to the park's Victorian bandstand or the loudspeakers from the political rallies taking place on the park's athletics track. India was (and is) a very noisy country with loudspeakers, honking horns, barking dogs and general crowd and traffic noise as a constant accompaniment to life. Surprisingly, it never really registered with us in terms of noise pollution as we had grown up with it and mentally relegated it to the background. But the influence of this background sound is pervasive—if I hear South Indian classical music it instantly takes me back to my childhood and gives me a feeling of real stillness.

Apparently the noise is getting worse. An account in The Times of London in March 2007 is headlined, "Horn chorus on the roads drives traffic police deaf." The story is about Bombay, and I quote:

> 'Horn OK please' is the car sticker of choice in India and a motto religiously adhered to on the frantic streets of Bombay. With vehicles jostling for the smallest gaps and pedestrians and animals crossing haphazardly, a driver in the country's biggest city never has a hand off the horn for long. The incessant hooting is taking its toll on the traffic police... With noise levels averaging more than 90 decibels—double the level deemed safe for urban areas by the World Health Organisation—most are partially deaf.
>
> "There is a cultural divide and you can't judge by Western standards," Mahesh Athvale, public relations officer at the Bombay Traffic Branch, said. "In the West blowing your horn is an insult, but here it is like people greeting each other."

> *Asked about the effect of noise pollution on his health, the unidentified officer on duty replied: "It's really noisy, I can barely hear you."*

I once stood on the wall next to the park in a line of pushing and shoving schoolboys to see the Russian leader, Khrushchev, go by in a noisy and exuberant motorcade. What the leader of the 'evil empire' was doing in small town Coimbatore I'll never know, but it was the time of India's love affair with Russia as a counterbalance to the influence of the West. The day was made more memorable by my brother John slipping off the wall and breaking his arm—undoubtedly the victim of a dastardly communist plot.

Every few years the wrestlers would come to town for a couple of weeks. These were professionals who toured the country. We had no idea at the time that it was all a fix and avidly bought the cheaply printed booklets with descriptions of our heroes and were eager for news of the results of each night's bouts. The big hero was an Indian called Dhara Singh—who always won, though not before he was apparently in theatrically serious danger of losing each bout. King Kong, a large, bald Eastern European, was the baddie, though we loved him. He visited the school once and amazed us by bending iron bars and lifting weights. There was, inevitably, a masked wrestler whom the others tried to unmask and never succeeded, though to keep the excitement levels up, they came pretty darn close. I wonder why we though it so important to unmask him as we didn't know him from Adam anyway! The one who most impressed was an oriental chap called Wong Buck Lee, whose speciality was the 'flying kick'. We practiced this for hours in the long jump pit—it was too dangerous to do it elsewhere as you risked a broken limb.

With the advent of the school holidays, the boarders left for home and the vast school grounds were left to the children of the teachers. There were two boys my age, let's call them Jacob and Matthew, the sons of a South Indian teacher. The father was a dark, squat Syrian Christian from Kerala, his wife was taller, pale and beautiful. Jacob, the elder son, took after his father and was a short, squint-eyed belligerent boy with spiky hair with whom I feuded more than played—he was the reason I got my canings. His mother applied a white cream called Afghan Snow to his face every day in the hope that it would improve his complexion. You can still buy the product in Asian corner shops—I can vouch for the fact that it didn't work on Jacob, but it left him with an interesting mildewed look. He seemed to resent the fact that my father was senior to his in the school, possibly reflecting the conversations that took place in his home. We sometimes fought, wrestling and punching each other. He gave me a wide berth for a while after I once chased him and flung a broken wooden *boochee* comb[1] at him, that hit him on the crown of his head and stuck in his scalp—he was terror struck because he thought I had damaged his brain and that he would die. No such luck.

The other brother, Matthew, was more like his mother, pleasant and even tempered and we got on well. We roamed the school grounds together all through the holidays, only popping back home for our meals. One summer, my father gave me an old golf club and a couple of golf balls. Matthew and I set up a golf course across the entire school grounds and hacked our way round it several times a day, walking miles in the process.

I also had a classmate, Ravi, who lived just across the road from the school. His house was screened by an elaborate garden in which grew fruit trees, mainly banana, watered by an irrigation system from their well. The orchard and streams provided us with hours of enjoyment, sailing our paper boats and playing hide and seek among the trees. When thirsty, we would be given 'pink' water from the well (probably laced with potassium permanganate, which our family also used liberally on any strawberries we received to ensure any harmful bacteria were

---

[1] 'boochee' means insect in Tamil. A boochee comb was a nit comb.

neutralised). Ravi's older brother, Madhu, went on to become an Admiral in the Indian Navy. Another friend's father was in the police, and had thoughtfully provided his son with a couple of no longer used but real police swords. We used these to stage elaborate recreations of fights we had seen in films and, fortunately, though I don't know how, managed to avoid kebabing each other!

The only other teachers left in school premises during the holidays were two lovely elderly spinsters, the Misses Nurse, who had a treasure trove of old junk they let us forage through—stereoscopes, coins, sharp and deadly Ghurkha knives—kukris—and old photographs. They fed us cakes and home made tamarind jam.

5
Family Life

Being young, my parents were quickly into the Coimbatore social scene and their evenings were spent in entertaining, visiting friends or going to the Coimbatore Club, leaving us children to be looked after by the ayah—this was not unusual for families in India. My father was tall, slim and good looking, with slicked-down black hair parted on the right, and a light olive complexion, which I inherited. He taught maths, physics and chemistry, but also had to take his turn supervising the boys' dormitories in the evenings. He had a natural authority about him; he'd been Head of his House at school and had commanded troops in the war, so the boys treated him with respect. Their nickname for him was George

Formby because he apparently looked like the actor and singer—this was lost on me as I had no idea at the time who this Formby was or what he did. When I did find out I could see a very faint resemblance, mainly based on hairstyle, though my father was much better looking and didn't have buck teeth. There is no evidence that he ever touched a ukulele.

My mother was, in contrast, very fair, almost florid, with light brown hair and blue eyes. She was good looking in a haughty sort of way. She was extremely self confident and could be very charming and popular when she wanted to be—as demonstrated by her wide circle of friends—but she could also be very tough and combative. She was a person of great principle, honest as they come, and quite prepared to speak her mind. As a teacher, and she was my Class Teacher for a year, she was respected because she was a very strict disciplinarian.

My parents' friends were drawn from the younger teachers and from the English managers of T. Stanes & Co., the coffee company. One of these was a man nicknamed 'Wolfie'. He drove an open topped Austin tourer, a novelty in those days (well, any one with a car then was a novelty), and took the family on weekend trips to the Nilgiri and Anaimalai Hills. Wolfie's thing was to wear a red fez and false plastic nose and glasses, looking like Groucho Marx, and to 'honk' his nose at the village girls we passed while sounding the car's horn. Ah, simple fun.

My relationship with my parents was mixed. My mother was not one for showing a great deal of affection—I can't ever remember being hugged—and she tended to offer more criticism than praise. I gave her a wide berth. My father was friendly and pleasant, very amusing when he was around though he was mostly at work. I can still picture him in his buff coloured cotton suit, white shirt and green tie—always green—striding across the playing field to come home for lunch. I had a reasonably good relationship with him as he could be an interesting companion, though a terrible tease and could sometimes take a prank too far. He once made a bamboo longbow and some blunt bamboo arrows, and decided it would be funny to try it out by shooting at my mother who was sitting in the next room doing her needlework. The arrow hit her squarely in the middle of the forehead—she wasn't expecting it and it must have hurt like hell. It was the only time I saw her weep uncontrollably.

He and I could be surprisingly close. He once took me on a memorable weekend trip through the backwaters of Kerala, well before it was discovered as a tourist spot. We spent our lunchtime in the bar of the Malabar Hotel on Willingdon Island, Cochin (now called Kochi) with its wonderful view of the harbour, watching the ships in port—the first time I had seen cargo ships close up. He drank beer and I drank shandy. Cochin is a trading port with a long history, stretching back to the time of King Solomon, when Arab, Phoenician and even Chinese traders came in search of spices like the precious pepper, cardamom and cloves, and ivory, silks and sandalwood from Mysore. Marco Polo, Vasco da Gama and the Dutch and British also came to trade, leaving a legacy of a population of Christians, Jews, Muslim and Hindus who live together peacefully today.

Dad and I spent the afternoon taking a country boat through the enchanting Kerala backwaters watching village life unfold along the banks. We passed temples and mosques and watched the fishermen manning their Chinese-style fishing nets, more fishing machines really, which worked on cantilevers and weights. We docked at a small town called Allepey and spent the night in a cheap creaky wooden hotel before travelling back to Cochin by bus the next morning and taking the train back to Coimbatore. Dad would also suddenly decide that I needed shoes or clothes, and whisk me off to the market—I think it was possibly an excuse to escape the household for a while.

I don't know why I was singled out, or how he managed to persuade my mother that he was going off with me for a weekend—we also went to the Periyar Dam together and took trips to the foothills of the Nilgiris. I was a quiet, curious child, very fond of reading and drawing—I read anything from the classics, to adventure novels, to comics; I even read the daily newspaper, the Madras Mail. I was not, however, a nerdy kid. I enjoyed playing games and sport, roamed the countryside, catapult in pocket to pick off the unwary wildlife, and was just a typical small boy taken with the wonderful delights on offer in the teemingly multi-cultural India of the 1950s. I think my father enjoyed educating me on our trips, and probably saw much of his childhood self in me. It was a bond that lasted the test of time and I remained closer to him than my brothers or sister until his death. My brother Wensley, who was the eldest, intelligent, good at games, good looking and very sociable, was really my mother's favourite until we were all demoted in our parent's affections for a time with the arrival of my sister.

The five year age difference between Wensley, and me meant that we had nothing in common and little to do with each other. He enjoyed sports and games, and liked to build things and tinker with the old Raleigh bicycle my father had bought for him from Dr Herman—the gears fascinated him. John and I were three years apart, so also had little in common, in fact we loathed each other and on more than one occasion he got a good past-ing from me, once with a cricket bat. He soon developed a strategy of baiting me until I grabbed him, when he would shout, 'Mum/Dad, Owen's hitting/hurting/bullying me,' at which point I would be scolded or punished. So revenge was taken when they were not around.

John was the golden child, with light brown to blond hair and he was spoiled rotten as he was the youngest. He was very fond of my mother and hated to have her out of his sight. His position was put in jeopardy by the arrival of my sister, Susan, in 1953, he was no longer the youngest child—and his place in my parents' affections had been taken by the longed-for daughter. I think it was a very traumatic time for him.

Social life in India in the 1950s and 60s was mainly centred on paying visits to each other at home, most often unannounced. Whenever we had visitors, which was at least once or twice a week, we children were banished from the sitting room, largely I think because the adults talked about school matters and gossiped about the other teachers. We didn't mind as the visitors were usually other teachers and we didn't particularly want to hang around them. If occasionally we were present and the conversation was straying into areas of gossip, my mother would call out, "Long ears!" to alert the visitors—and we were sensitive enough to take this as a hint—well, we'd have been thick-skinned not to—and disappear.

Inevitably, we spent a lot of the time in the care of the servants while my parents got on with their work and social lives. This did not mean we were unhappy—far from it. We were free to do whatever we wished outside the house and there were few constraints on us. Home was where we came for our meals or to sleep. We didn't know any better and all our friends appeared to have similar arms-length relationships with their folks. It was a pretty safe environment in which to grow up and we had the extensive school grounds and the nearby park as our playground.

The best times with my parents were on some evenings when we would sit out in the front garden of our isolated bungalow, with a large enamel pot of coffee, Stanes coffee naturally, drinking it, watching the sun go down and talking into the evening. We would watch the twilight do its sudden quick change into night over Coimbatore and sit in the warm darkness, looking up at the sky and listening to the evening sounds of the town and the insect sounds around us. We would talk about the stars, which were brightly visible as there wasn't so much light pollution then, discuss the origins of the universe, our relatives and the history of the Raj—my father would talk about Sir Henry Lawrence, his school's founder, and the other heroes of British India. Looking up at the stars on these clear nights gave even a young child like me "brilliant evidence of the awful loneliness, of the hopeless obscure insignificance of our globe lost in the splendid revelation of a glittering, soulless universe" (Joseph Conrad, in his novel, Chance). These were rare and deeply satisfying moments.

There was a ritual at the end of the scholastic year when the dreaded examination results were due along with the critical decisions on whether we would be promoted to the next class. My parents, being teachers, obviously knew our results in advance and for a week or two before they were to be announced would mischievously torment us by implying that we had done badly, outlining what the dire consequences would be. They did this knowing well that Wensley and I were generally top of the class—John tended to be at the other end—and thought it all a huge joke. This raised our anxiety levels and we went about in a blue funk until the day came when we had to go in to collect our report forms and found to our relief that we had done well. Despite this, we fell for this trick over and over again.

We were disciplined. Punishment, when we did offend, was generally short and sharp—a whack with the hand or any suitable object lying around. We were never 'grounded'—the word did not exist—and it was useless to deny us pocket money or privileges as we had none.

A lot of our companionship came from the ayahs who

looked after us—some of them just a few years older than we were. At one point we had an Anglo-Indian nanny, let's call her Noreen, who stayed with us for a year or two. She was mainly employed to look after my sister, Susan. Noreen had fallen on hard times. She was estranged from her husband, destitute, and had two small girls living free at boarding school in the local convent, she must have been in her early thirties. One of the storerooms was cleared to give her a bedroom. We loved climbing on to Noreen's bed where she told us stories and off-colour jokes—known then as 'Pat yarns' as there was usually an Irishman called Pat involved in risqué business. She also told us about her life and difficulties with her husband. It was the first time that an adult had treated us as equals and shown us lots of affection and we appreciated it. It jarred that Noreen was required to call my parents 'Sir' and 'Madam' as I regarded her as one of the family. I think that in some small way it shaped my attitude towards my own domestic servants later in life, treating them as equals and earning their loyalty in return.

Noreen came to us because my father was the Secretary of the church's Friend In Need Society. The society provided charitable help and American supplied powdered milk, butter and cheese to the parish's poor Anglo-Indians. Many of these goodies were stored in our larder as my father was required to keep a stock to hand out to people who turned up at our house after hours because they were in desperate need of assistance. We had a regular stream of callers and we children became used to handling them. One day when opening the door to with a sad-looking, balding, middle-aged white man in creased white shirt and khaki shorts that were too big for him, I announced loudly to my father, 'There's a chap here from the Friend in Need Society'. This turned out to be Uncle Bob (to be fair, I had never seen him before) who was Chief Engineer responsible for signalling on the Indian Railways and a very big cheese indeed. Bob took it very well—even when he suffered further indignity when my brother John, peering up the leg of his voluminous shorts, saw something interesting and grabbed.

Bob, who was married to my mother's aunt, Dolly, a large and large-hearted woman, travelled in style on the railway when he was on his inspection tours. He had his own suite of carriages—sitting room cum dining room, bedroom, bathroom and kitchen. He would sit on a little balcony in the end carriage, in one of those teak planters' chairs, waving like a monarch on a state visit to the workers respectfully lined up to offer their salaams as he went along. The nice thing about Uncle Bob was that he was a really unpretentious boffin. He loved making electrical gadgets and home movies and, with pipe firmly clenched in his teeth, was a man of few words.

Some of his reticence was possibly grief for his son Bobby who, through illness, was confined to a wheelchair and could not speak. There was nothing wrong with young Bobby's mind though, and he would sometimes grunt and correct his father if he got something wrong as he constructed his electrical gadgets—and Bob would occasionally tease his son and test his knowledge by deliberately getting it wrong. Bob and Dolly also had a younger daughter, Margaret, who was healthy and effervescent and took care to ensure that her brother was looked after. Margaret still looks after her brother's interests and Bobby has defied all the odds and is still alive in India at nearly 60 years old.

We never saw anything of my father's relatives. My mother's lived mainly in Bangalore and we went there one Christmas to stay with my grandmother, who was matron of Bishop Cotton's Girls School. Granny Arklie had been widowed young, leaving her with eight children—seven girls and one boy. One of the girls died young and another, Phyllis was wheelchair bound because of polio. Unfortunately, the only boy, Gerald, was killed by the Japanese in Burma during the Chindit campaign in WW II. Granny got national publicity when she went one morning to call on Mrs Drayton, Headmistress of the school, only to find her gruesomely murdered in a blood spattered room. The murderer was caught, he was a former school servant who had tried to rob Mrs Drayton, and Granny was called as the main witness at the trial—reported in grisly detail by the Madras Mail.

The other daughters, my aunts, lived in Bangalore—though one of them, Colleen, had gone to live in England. The youngest daughter, Shirley, was very beautiful—and had a sharp business brain. She eventually married John Webb, the heir to Webb's Garage in Bangalore, and subsequently took over the business when he died. Barbara, was married to a race horse trainer, Rex Shaw, and Joan, about whom more later on, married Ronnie Lakin, a navigator in the Indian Air Force.

My first visit to Bangalore since being born there was not a great success. I was too young at the time to have had any recollection of the place. My parents had talked about the dances at the Bowring Institute, the hub of social activity, and Cubbon Park and Lalbagh Gardens—in which, incidentally, the British installed a copy of the London Crystal Palace. I was dragged along to see the sights and to attend a 'Christmas Tree' in the Bowring Institute. I managed to crack a tooth on a shotgun pellet while eating snipe that someone had shot and presented to us, and on Christmas Day, pleased with my new toy cap pistol, pointed it at a passing Scottie dog who, undaunted and no doubt thinking me impertinent, decided to attack me. I ran, dropping the pistol which, as it was made of cast iron, broke when it hit the concrete floor. Bangalore is now one of India's fastest developing cities and a centre for information technology. It has become overdeveloped and polluted and has lost a lot of its charm. It became a magnet for retiring Anglo-Indians who retired to Whitefields—a friend cruelly described it as God's Waiting Room—where they settled in the bungalows and houses, spending their days in socialising and tending their gardens till the time came for them to 'fall face down in the curry'.

As teachers, my parents were not highly paid, my father got 250 Rupees a month, my mother would have got about 150—this amounted to an equivalent of about £20 per month as a family income in the early 1950s. By comparison, our servants were paid between 15 and 30 Rupees a month, so money did go far and of course my parents were not paying for their accommodation. A lot of the children we knew as friends came from wealthy families. One close friend, Rajan, lived in a brand new two-storied house outside the school boundary, about a hundred yards down the road from ours. His father had something to do with growing and selling peanuts on an industrial scale because the house contained a couple of large rooms piled high with sacks of raw peanuts on which we played, building fortifications out of them. Occasionally, Rajan's dad would send our family a sack of peanuts and we would eat them fried, roasted in hot sand in a *karai*[1] or boiled—they go rubbery when boiled but are very tasty with salt, green chillies and chopped onions.

Rajan's story is an interesting one. When I first met him he was a weedy, shy child, his initial attraction was that he possessed a bicycle on which I wished to learn to ride. Gradually our friendship grew and we went everywhere—he was a timid boy and did not much like rough games and was scared of the local chokras—but was a good stooge, a Robin to my Batman. Then one day I was told that he was very ill and that I would not see him for some time. It turned out that he had contracted smallpox and that he had got it badly. There were doubts as to whether he would survive. My parents did not know that I used to visit his house to enquire after him—they would not have allowed it as they were terrified of anyone in our family catching smallpox. I would stand at the gate and speak to Rajan's sister Jayshree, a couple of years older than him, who used to give me updates on his health and pass my messages to him—gossip from school and a bit of encouragement.

He pulled through, but even then I was not allowed to visit him. When he finally emerged at school months later, his face was badly scarred and he was, unsurpris-

---

[1] the Indian equivalent of a wok.

ingly, even thinner and weaker. But something strange happened. As he got stronger he seemed to fill out and become more thickset—and to my astonishment his personality also seemed to change and he became noticeably bolder and tougher. He did not understand why—but a different Rajan emerged. He got the usual cruel insults from other children about his pock-marked face and instead of accepting them mildly as he would have done in the past, he became quite aggressive. It was as though nature had robbed him of his looks but had compensated him by strengthening his personality. He sometimes became devil-may-care to the point of danger and the local chokras started to be very wary of him. Rajan remained a close friend—with me he was the most loyal friend—and you'll hear more about him when he surfaced later in my life.

While Rajan's people were rich, my introduction to the world of the 'super rich' came from my occasional trips across the road from the school to the factory complex of an industrialist called G D Naidu to play with his son, who was receiving private tuition from my father. The son, who was about 14 years old, used to drive me round the complex at speed in an old blue racing car—which in later years I recognised might have been a Bugatti. G D Naidu was a hugely wealthy industrialist, sometimes referred to as the Edison of India. His businesses covered electrical, mechanical, agricultural and automotive engineering, and he ran a bus company. It was said that he had once met Hitler and taken a photograph of him. The story goes that G D had once imported a new Cadillac from America but, faced with a demand that he pay the extortionate duty required, which would more than double the cost of the car, he chose not to abandon it to the Government but took a sledgehammer to it.

Every Christmas, those wealthy parents who wanted to ensure that the school looked favourably upon their children, or who were thankful that their children had done well in their exams, would send baskets of fruit and Indian sweets all artfully decorated in coloured tissue paper to the teachers, including our parents. Concealed in the middle of the basket would be the real gift, cartons of foreign cigarettes or a bottle of hard to come by Scotch whisky. My father, along with his other teacher colleagues, never turned these away, it was an established custom and the parents would have been deeply offended if their gift had been refused.

My parents, in common with many people those days, were heavy smokers. We kids were frequently asked in the evenings to go the three-quarter mile round trip in the dark to buy them cigarettes from the local 'kudday', or shop, if they had run out—my father smoked about 40 a day, packets of Star cigarettes or tins of Berkeley, my mother half that. The shop was nothing more than a crude shed, lit by kerosene lamps, and doubled as the shopkeeper's home. I demanded, and frequently got, one anna (12 annas to the Rupee, 20 Rupees to the £ back then) as my tip from my parents for carrying out this task. This paid for a pocketful of peanuts and a cube or two of *jaggery* (compacted brown sugar) which together are a superb combination, known to us boys as 'jigs[1] and jags'.

We were rarely ill, which was fortunate as the treatment of illness was, by the standards of today, quite rudimentary. Cuts were treated with iodine—which stings painfully—or mercurochrome, a scarlet liquid which doesn't. No prizes for guessing which we preferred. The standard treatment for an illness was bed rest and if you had lost your appetite you were fed on thin liquid arrowroot, which is quite horrible, or on 'pish-pash' a sort of rice and dhal (lentil) paste designed really for infants, invalids or the elderly without teeth! The doctor was called only in real emergencies; I can remember two. Once when I developed sores on my ankles from playing in a sandpit and the infection made the glands in my groin so painful that I couldn't walk. The doctor came and gave me an antibiotic injection. The second time was more serious: my father had found out when serving in

---

[1] In South India peanuts were known to us boys as jignuts or 'jigs'.

Malaya that he was allergic to penicillin, which had resulted in his hospitalisation there for several months. In Coimbatore he cut himself playing tennis and applied a proprietary ointment which, unknown to him contained penicillin. He broke out in huge weeping blisters and had to call in the doctor, who confined him to bed for two months and treated him regularly, mainly it seems by applying gentian violet to the blisters. This stuff got all over the place and covered his bed linen in purple blotches. We never succeeded in getting it off.

Some Sundays we were given doses of castor oil to keep our bowels regular—it was the most awful tasting stuff and you had to remain within close proximity to a toilet for the rest of the day. I was once given an oil bath—massaged with warm *gingelly* (sesame) oil and then given a hot bath, something unheard of in Coimbatore's warm climate. I slept the sleep of the dead for hours afterwards as it was so relaxing. It was not unusual for children at school to be absent for the day because they had been given an 'oil bath'; it seemed a regular part of their routine. Once when I developed a rash, I was given a neem bath, warm water in which leaves from the neem tree[1] had been steeped, which was supposed to have medici-

---

1   Neem—Azadirachta Indica, has long been known for its healing properties. Discovered by the West in 1959—we were using it long before then.

nal properties. To keep fit, my father took regular doses of Sanatogen Nerve Tonic—a mustardy smelling white powder which was mixed with water. He was always very thin and energetic.

All the fresh air, exercise and exposure to Coimbatore's bacteria probably kept me quite healthy. I could spend hours outside, barefoot, whacking stones with a piece of plank pretending I was Len Hutton (England's cricket captain) playing cricket for England against India or Australia. This usually involved my giving an audible commentary, and I also frequently talked to myself while playing, which led my father to conclude that I 'talked to the trees'. When my parents went on their trips with Wolfie, or later to visit Wensley at boarding school in Montfort, I usually declined, preferring to stay at home on my own and be pampered by cook and ayah. I somehow felt that I was not really part of the family. I was more introspective than they were, very fond of books and of drawing and writing stories and of 'planning' impossible projects. I would agree to go on the occasional special treat to, of all places, the railway station to visit the newspaper stall of Higginbottoms, where I would be allowed a couple of Mickey Mouse comics—remember, this was the only English bookshop in our town. Then on to the India Coffee House for an iced coffee and freshly made hot potato crisps (called 'potato chips' in India).

The family usually walked there and back—a fair old distance—we did not own a car and neither of my parents could drive.

In the UK, when in her 50s, my mother inexplicably passed her driving test, and bought a large red Vauxhall car. I always knew when she was coming to visit when I heard the angry tooting of horns of the frustrated drivers behind her as she drove at a steady and cautious 29 mph, just under the speed limit, my father in the passenger seat beside her with a large map open so he could navigate for her—though they were entirely familiar with the route which was about three miles from where they lived. I once caught my father polishing this car with a Brillo wire-wool pan scourer—so little did they know about automobiles.

We spent our summer holidays in Ooty in the Nilgiri Hills (*neela giri* in Tamil means 'blue mountains') with the redoubtable Mr Maude. This was the place to cool off from the heat of the plains as temperatures rarely rise above 77 degrees Fahrenheit in the summer—and can be down to freezing during the nights in winter. I preferred making the trip by train, the Blue Mountain Railway, a scenic, narrow gauge 'toy train' working on a rack and pinion to stop it sliding back down the slopes, that wound its way round the hills from Mettupalayam via Coonoor and Lovedale to Ooty. I did on a couple of occasions go to Ooty via a tortuous car journey up the twisting hill roads guaranteed to bring on motion sickness, with which I suffered. Mr Maude had a very English mock-Tudor bungalow, called Fairview, perched on the side of a hill, and owned a highly polished maroon Morris car, so highly polished that the undercoat shone through in places (maybe they were using Brillo pads too). He seemed pleased to have us there as he lived alone, with his servants—I always wondered whether he had a soft spot for my mother. We made daily trips in the car to the market—known as the Shandy—to buy our meat and veg, and went via the railway crossing called Charing Cross (it is still there).

The town had a very English feel to it, with houses that would not have looked out of place in England dotted around the hillside, a fine church on a hill and Breeks Memorial School, run on public school lines with the pupils dressed in maroon blazers and caps. St Stephen's Church, a Victorian gothic pile, is thought to have been built using timber from the palace of Tipu Sultan[1] in Seringapatam—and hauled up the hills using elephants.

---

1 Tipu Sultan (1750-1799), known as the Tiger of Mysore, was a Muslim ruler in a largely Hindu domain. He posed a threat to the British in South India and had imprisoned over 200 captured British, who were held in conditions of great cruelty. He was killed defending his capital.

Ooty was surrounded by beautiful green eucalyptus, tea and spice plantations—cinnamon, cloves and cardamom—and by downland across which the Ooty hunt, in their blue coats, galloped after jackals rather than foxes—sadly no longer, I understand. The cool climate was a novelty—we had to wear warm clothing and cover up with blankets at night. On good afternoons we would venture into the eucalyptus plantations to see the workers distilling eucalyptus oil, or to explore the strange 'egg house', an egg-shaped folly that could be seen from the road leading into Ooty. In the evenings, after dinner we would talk round the sitting room fireplace. It was where I learned about the ill-fated Mallory and Irvine Everest expedition (both mountaineers went missing after setting out for the summit of Everest. Mallory's body was found recently, but there is still debate over whether they were the first to reach the summit). My own mountaineering, or rather hill-climbing achievement was to trek to the top of Mount Dodabetta, about 8,000 Ft. I also got to visit the famously snooty Ooty Club, founded in 1830 and not so snooty now, whose claim to fame is that it is where snooker was invented. On Saturdays I would go with my father to the horse racing. My father liked a flutter, and we would sit on the side of the hill and watch the races, leaving a confetti trail of failed bets in our wake when we left.

One of the curiosities of Ooty is the Toda people. I first saw them at the Botanical Gardens, where they had an encampment. The Todas are a race of indigenous tribespeople, quite different from the local population, and were the original inhabitants of Ooty. In 1823, the then Collector of Coimbatore, a chancer called John Sullivan, took a fancy to their lands and bought them for the magnificent sum of one Rupee! Bargain or rip-off—you decide! A European visitor in the 1840s perpetuated the myth that the Todas were an offshoot of the Lost Tribe of Israel because he declared that, "In dress and stature [the Todas] strongly resemble characters from the Old Testament". Intensive studies have proved them to be of Dravidian (ie. South Indian) descent even though they are tall and fair, unlike the wiry and dark-skinned Tamil people, and have a distinctive language and customs. For example, they worshipped the sacred buffalo and practised polyandry—a woman would become a wife to several brothers. They lived in distinctive huts called 'munds'—but are increasingly now losing their distinct identity and live in normal houses. It is estimated that there are only around 1,000 Todas left today.

Back down on the plains after a summer in Ooty, we looked forward in October to Divali, known in the South as Deepavali, the festival of fireworks and lights that celebrates the homecoming of the hero of the Ramayana,

Rama, and his wife Sita. This is the time when millions of homes are illuminated with small terracotta oil lamps and there are exuberant firework displays—we called them crackers, not fireworks. The festival runs for five days. Day 1 is the celebration of the home. Day 2 is to have your sins absolved. Day 3 is for puja to the goddess Lakshmi. Day 4 is the Hindu New Year. And Day 5 is brother and sister day, when gifts are exchanged. In addition to fireworks, large quantities of Indian sweets are eaten and there is lavish hospitality, which in India must include three essential elements: good food, good conversation and good music. Even the poorest Indian peasant will offer you the best food he has got—he would be ashamed to do otherwise. The Deepavali days of fireworks lead to serious air pollution but a positive aspect to this is that it also kills millions of malarial mosquitoes.

One or other of my wealthier Indian classmates usually invited me to his home for a Deepavali party—there was lavish entertainment, magicians, jugglers and even rides on an elephant one year. We ate our weight in sticky sweets: *ladoos, jelabis* and *burfees,* and then took part in the fireworks display, the highlight of which was the thunderous explosions of 'atom bombs'. Of course the run up to Deepavali was an opportunity for us schoolboys to let off fireworks during the breaks at school. A very popular and dangerous jape was to place an 'atom bomb' under an upturned enamel basin, pinched from the bathrooms in the boys' dormitory, to see how high it could be blown. I particularly liked the 'aeroplane crackers' which were sealed metal cylinders, the size of a thimble, with a small hole in the side through which the wick was inserted. The hole also functioned like a jet engine and as the gunpowder mixture ignited inside, the jet corkscrewed the cracker high into the air with a whizzing sound. They were highly unpredictable and could go in any direction—which of course was the attraction for us kids. No one was ever hit by one, it would have been like being struck by a bullet, but they came down red-hot as I found to my cost when I picked one up and blistered my fingers.

Christmas was of course the biggest festival of the year for us Anglo-Indians—the Indians enthusiastically celebrated it too. At Christmas, Granny Arklie in Bangalore would make Christmas cakes in cut down Dalda tins (Dalda was a vegetable oil), send them to the local bakery to be baked, and send these to us with generous quantities of kul kuls (a sugary coated pastry rolled on a fork) and a peculiar spicy, non-alcoholic but chilli-hot drink called 'otee'. We had a large Christmas tree, which was usually liberally decorated with cotton wool snow. Wensley says that this was sometimes simply a branch from a neem tree, at other times a proper fir—I was probably too young to tell the difference or too excited to care. My father always planted the fir tree in the garden after Christmas in the hope that it would grow, which of course it didn't as it had no roots and the climate was too hot. Each of us children received one Christmas present, and a gift-wrapped matchbox containing a couple of Rupees. One year I received a pop gun which fired a cork on a string. I kept this under my pillow for months just in case a burglar should break in. We children saved our occasional tips from the trips to buy cigarettes to buy my parents gifts: my father usually received a packet of cigarettes or box of matches and my mother a handkerchief or needles and pins.

We were also enrolled in the annual 'Christmas Tree' at Woodlands Hotel, one of a chain of hotels (they still exist). Masses of children attended one afternoon around Christmastime and had games, high tea and then present- giving by Father Christmas. My father was Father Christmas one year and took on the role so enthusiastically that he had an expensive pair of black knee-length boots made to go with his costume. He never ever wore these boots again! One year I received a plastic umbrella which, though I was pleased with it, was a strange present to give a seven or eight year old boy in December in a place where it only really rained during the summer monsoon.

In the spring, the festival of *'martu pongal'* would be

celebrated, a puja dedicated to the sacred cow—when all the cows would have their horns painted in bright colours. Spring also brought the kite-flying season, when we would be busy making our kites and spent much of our time in the sun flying them.

In around 1955 things changed for us. The Headmaster of Stanes School, Mr Fowler, went off to America for a couple of years to train for the priesthood. My father became acting Headmaster. We moved into the Headmaster's House, and the Headmaster's wife moved to our bungalow. The new house was palatial compared to the bungalow—two storeys, very large rooms, a huge enclosed garden, a big servants' block and a carpenter's shed, complete with resident school carpenter. We children were thrilled. There were some similarities to the bungalow we had left: we still had thunder boxes and the upstairs verandahs had been enclosed with plywood and windows to make extra rooms. Of course John and I ended up sleeping here.

Wensley had been packed off to boarding school in Montfort—one of the Quadrangular Sports schools. The reason was that, in order to pass the High School Examination, pupils had to pass in a second language—and Wensley found it difficult to get to grips with Tamil. Montfort offered French as an alternative, so off he went. He was growing up fast and, given the five year gap between us, the gap in understanding was now even wider. Rock and roll had come to India in the form of the film Rock around the Clock, with Bill Hayley and the Comets making a big impression. There were tales of Anglo-Indian customers jiving in the cinema aisles all over India. Wensley took to all of this in a big way and developed a deep liking for the songs of Elvis Presley (I was more of an Everly Brothers fan). I remember that he began to affect a turquoise cardigan with the collar hiked up, highly inappropriate and decidedly uncomfortable in tropical Coimbatore.

About this time, John too was developing strange habits. Shortly after dinner each evening, while the family talked or listened to the radio, he would fall soundly asleep—which led him to be nicknamed 'The Python'. If we were lucky, he would sleepwalk, getting up, walking across the room to do something aimless, then return to his chair to continue his sleep. Another of his strange habits was less amusing. In the middle of the night he would begin screaming—and I mean really terrified screams—as he suffered nightmares. My parents would usually rush to wake him, comfort him and then put him back to sleep. I got so used to this that I soon slept through the commotion. John cannot remember what the nightmares were about and really does not have any recollection of screaming.

In the two years that we lived in the big house, my parents upped the entertainment of their friends as their new home was now big enough in which to throw some really good parties. We began having people over to stay—among the first was the Anglo-Indian leader and MP, Frank Anthony, who paid us a state visit. During his visit we were forbidden entry to half the house and had to ensure we had our meals separate from the visitors. We children were glad when he left. All of this entertaining gave me an aversion to chickens for a while as I went to the kitchen block one day to find the cook cutting the throats of half a dozen chickens to serve them up for dinner. Fascinated by this in the grisly way that boys are, I stayed on to watch him and his assistant pluck and gut the birds—and this turned me off chicken for a while.

With all of their high profile entertaining, my parents were more popular than ever and we children enjoyed the increased space in the house—having a staircase was a novelty—and played in the large garden. The carpenter could be easily persuaded to make us superior and realistic wooden swords and my father found an antique gun with eight barrels from somewhere which he gave us to play with. It would be worth a fortune now if only we hadn't destroyed it. We were enjoying life and the notion of going back to our bungalow when the Headmaster returned was too difficult to contemplate.

My parents clearly thought so too as, in 1957, just before the Headmaster's return from America, they surprised us with the news that we were not going back to the bungalow after all. Instead, we packed up and left Coimbatore for Madras, where my father was to be the new Headmaster of St George's School—formerly the Civil Orphan Asylum.

6

The Orphanage

St George's School, Madras can lay claim to being the oldest western style school in India. It had started out in the 1680s in Fort St. George[1] as a place to house the orphan children of British soldiers of the East India Company killed in southern India and moved to the present site in Poonamallee High Road in the 1900s. Elements of its Raj association and orphanage status were everywhere. It took in large numbers of poor and orphaned Anglo-Indian children, many of whom had

---

[1] Fort St George also housed Robert Clive—Clive of India—who was responsible for firmly establishing British influence in India. He became one of the richest men in England from the payments made to him by Indian princes. He committed suicide.

foreign 'sponsors' and also had a sizeable contingent of fee-paying Indian children attracted by the European style education.

Every pupil, on entry as a boarder (which initially I was not) had all personal possessions removed and was issued with a complete set of school clothing, bedding in a canvas roll and a tin plate and mug stamped with his or her number. The dormitories were empty of all furniture and pupils brought out their bedding at night and slept where they liked in groups of friends. Toothpaste (round cakes of pink Gibbs dentifrice nailed to a wooden block) and soap (big chunks of red Lifebuoy) were communal. Meals were pretty basic—thick slice of bread, a banana and coffee for breakfast, watery curry, rice and dhal for lunch and dinner, mug of tea and bread for tea. All meals were served on your tin plate and mug, which you were required to wash up afterwards. Shoes were only worn when pupils went outside the school—so everyone went barefoot. The two school houses were Clive (after Robert Clive—red stripe on your vest) and Hastings (after Warren Hastings—blue stripe). I was in Hastings.

Pupils were only educated up to Standard Nine. This was part of the old orphanage ethos of only educating the orphans to a minimum standard to enable them to go on to earn a living. The boys usually joined the railways, police, armed services or post and telegraph department; the girls might go in for nursing or secretarial work—in the past, many of the girls were considered by then to be of marriageable age and there was always a queue of would-be suitors to take them off the orphanage's hands. Even in my day, some boys and girls left after the Ninth Standard to start earning a living. Those pupils who were more academic could go on to do their High School or Senior Cambridge exams, but had to do so at Doveton Corrie School, to which many of them cycled (wearing shoes, of course).

The school was situated on one bank of the Cooum River, the other bank contained the burning ghats for cremating Hindu dead. The sickly sweet smell of these cremations was ever present. The edges of the boys' playing field were waterlogged because of the river, and the little pools dotted around contained an interesting assortment of crabs. As we played our games barefoot, crabs were a hazard—not many schools can claim that.

We moved there in 1957 to a large, gloomy red-brick house with a big tope of trees behind it, mainly mango and banyan, which were inhabited by civet cats, who gave off a pungent smell. The house had an uncomfortable air about it, as though some terrible tragedy had taken place there. Wensley was convinced that it was haunted and would dash at speed past a particular upstairs corridor that felt very oppressive. The whole set-up, school, house, barefoot children, cremations and the miasma from the river combined to produce a morbid and musty feel. It did not help that we arrived just after one of the pupils had been bitten by a rabid dog, contracted rabies ('lockjaw') and died, which cast its own pall over the school.

Wensley, who had done well in his High School and Senior Cambridge exams, was enrolled in Loyola College to do his Pre-University course. John and I joined classes in St George's.

The school had two major attractions: it had a swimming pool and a fine brass band. Learning how to swim and, more importantly, trying to watch the girls swim (as few had costumes) was a major preoccupation of the boys. The only vantage point was high in the eaves of the boys' dormitory and there was a heavy demand for ringside seats. I learned to swim in this pool. I joined the school band, which was then the only National Cadet Corps (NCC) band in India. It went every year to Delhi to take part in the 26th January Republic Day parade. My parents thought it would be useful for me to learn to play an instrument so I went along. I think I got preferential treatment because I was the Headmaster's son, and probably leapfrogged a queue of more talented and deserving children wanting to join.

Mr Fritchley, the Bandmaster, a lovely, patient man, small and with a toothbrush moustache and glasses, decided I should learn to play the clarinet, so I squeaked my way through lessons. Though I learned the basics and could knock out a tune, I never really mastered the instrument or the ability to read music. When the band played in public I mimed. The canny Fritchley soon realised I wasn't up to it and moved me on to playing the cymbals. This was a marching band, I was a puny 11 year old, but I managed—just.

We took on a lot of private gigs, playing at weddings and functions. We would wear our colourful full dress uniform and travel to the venues in the back of one of the school's windowless delivery vans, an ancient, rattling vehicle used to collect supplies from the bazaar. Sitting on the floor, which was covered with a dhurrie to protect our uniforms, we would sing a medley of World War II barrack room songs such as Quartermaster's Stores, Long Way to Tipperary ("It's a long way to tickle Mary") and the White Cliffs of Dover. We also sang witty doggerel songs (well, witty for us schoolboys) like:

> 'One day I went out hunting,
> I had to carry a gun,
> And what do you think they gave me?
> Some coffee and a bun!

> The coffee that they gave me
> Was worse than charcoal water,
> And who do you think it was made by?
> By Mrs So-and-So's daughter.' (A suitable name would be inserted).

There were ruder and more scurrilous songs, too filthy to repeat here: 'Mrs Brown I love your daughter' (the only clean line in the whole song) and 'I love a lassie, a bloody great Madrassi' being examples. And we altered the words to Old Macdonald had a Farm to be less than complimentary about our teachers. How the admirable Fritchley, who sat in the front passenger seat, never heard us, I'll never know. We were probably drowned out by that all pervasive Indian noise of cars, buses, trams, braying loudspeakers and the rattling of the van.

We also did occasional weekend NCC camps. Our function was mainly to play at the parades as the various NCC contingents from local schools and colleges marched past. The show would be livened up with battlefield demonstrations by the college cadets—who would charge out of a smokescreen with fixed bayonets, screaming bloodcurdling yells in adolescent voices that had recently broken so that it sounded more like an attack by swarthy Swiss yodellers. The food however was excellent. Lashings of rice and *sambar*, with *pappadums*, and a man who came round with a shiny brass bucket full of warm ghee[1], which he ladled liberally over your grub. We ate sitting cross-legged on the floor, using our fingers. "*Rombo nullah*", as we would say in Tamil—'very nice'—and you had to wobble your head from side to side in the South Indian way[2].

Madras was an interesting city, full of historical and natural features. The East India Company had its first bases (its factories) there and Fort St George has a lot of artefacts from the Raj. I also made a trip to St Thomas Mount, where St Thomas—'doubting Thomas'—was killed eight years after he arrived in India around 52 to 72 AD. The Madras beaches are wonderful, with strong surf that makes it challenging to swim in—as I found out having only just learned to swim. I spent more time scraping the bottom of the beach as the surf tumbled me round. The earliest British visitors to Madras were rowed to the beach in country boats from the sailing vessels in which they had survived the six month long trip from Britain. This last part was very dangerous because of the raging surf and there were those who unfortunately drowned within sight of their destination.

---

1   Clarified butter, used in food and for religious ceremonies—delicious but very fattening heart-attack food.

2   Apparently, the only other culture to indicate approval by shaking the head is the Hungarians.

The family made frequent trips to Moore Market, near the Central Station, sometimes simply to revel in the sheer variety of stuff on offer after small-town Coimbatore. Sadly, Moore Market was destroyed by fire in 1985.

But the highlight for me was the family's regular visits to the Hotel Dasprakash for their exquisite paper-thin ghee *dosais*[1*]—I have never tasted anything better since. It is still there and I gather that their *dosais* continue to be famous.

Everything seemed to be going well. Uncle Bob (big cheese from the Railway, remember?) and his family lived in Madras and we visited them from time to time—he would pick us up in his 'sit up and beg' Austin, with the stuffing coming out of the worn leather seats. We participated in his home movies and somewhere there is a sequence of me in my best band uniform, clutching the redundant clarinet, but thankfully not attempting to play it. The news on the band front was that I would be accompanying them to the Republic Day parade in Delhi.

Glamorous Aunt Shirl, my mother's youngest sister, turned up to visit, boyfriend John in tow in a red 1930s

---

1   Dosai is a pancake made from a batter of fermented rice and lentils, common in South India. It is filled with spiced potato and eaten with sambar, a thin lentil curry, and coconut chutney, often off a banana leaf.

MG sports car. We met sundry aunts, more distant relations of my mother's, one of them so enormous that it was said she had to take her own chair to the cinema. And Granny Arklie visited from Bangalore and spent a few weeks with us. It was my first chance to get to know her well, and she used to get up early to see me off to band practice—but not before making me a cup of instant coffee—yup, it had taken hold—diluted with condensed milk. I had never tasted coffee so good and, even now, I sometimes treat myself to coffee with evaporated milk; condensed milk would, I think, be a step too far for my ageing arteries.

Then, disaster! My father resigned six months into the job. We children knew something was up because of the increase in agitated conversations between my parents and the fragments of information that indicated all was not well. I am still not entirely clear what happened, but it must have been serious because Dad resigned and had no job to go to. My parents decided to move to Bangalore, to lodge with my mother's relatives, while they looked for fresh employment. "Oh no", I thought, "Here we go again!" I was not ready for more change, having just settled in to a new school and made new friends. There, I thought, went my chance of going to the Republic Day parade. However, I needn't have worried on that score. It suited my parents to park me in the school as a boarder over December and January of 1957/58 as it meant having one less child to accommodate in Bangalore while they sorted themselves out.

So there I was in the Christmas holidays, living in school as a boarder with a few other children who were either orphans or whose parents could not have them home for whatever reason. It was absolutely great! We roamed the grounds, climbed the trees, swam in the pool, killed and ate the occasional sparrow roasted in a cigarette tin over a campfire, and generally indulged ourselves. It was my first Christmas away from home. My parents sent me a parcel of Christmas food—those were the days when parcels were wrapped in white cotton cloth, sewn, and the seams protected with blobs of sealing wax. Being generous, I offered to share it with some of the boys. I had forgotten that most of then had never had much in their lives and they fell on the food like a pack of hungry wolves—I found myself fighting to get my share.

In early January, joined by the other boys in the band, I made the long trip of over a thousand miles by rail from Madras to Delhi. The journey took three nights and two days but we enjoyed it immensely. We saw India go by in its huge variety: fields, jungles, towns, mountains and rivers. We arrived at strange and exotic stations in the early hours and watched them come alive with vendors of unusual foods and novelties, which we bargained for from the windows of our carriage. Our meals were delivered at stations down the line having been ordered hundreds of miles before and telegraphed forward—my favourite food was 'curd bath' which was yoghurt and rice mixed together, slightly spiced, and served in a banana leaf. We band boys occupied a Third Class carriage to ourselves—Fritchley had wisely moved elsewhere—and we enjoyed each other's company with no adults around to set the rules.

The Republic Day parade was a huge affair. Contingents from all the armed services and Cadet Corps were billeted in a tented camp outside Delhi in the Cantonment. The tents were bitterly cold in the Delhi winter. We were under army discipline and rose at reveille and stood to attention (even if unfortunate enough to be on the toilet) at sunset as the 'Last Post' sounded and the national flag came down. We queued for enormous meals of every description as they had to cater for people from all over India. Chapattis were a novelty to us rice-eating southerners, so we stacked them high on our plates. Many of us packed handfuls of chapattis in our kitbags before we left Delhi and we ate them for days afterwards back in Madras. By then they were as brittle as crisps.

During the day we marched and marched and marched as the parade was rehearsed. The soles of my feet, in my badly fitting new boots, became so painful that I could only walk on the outside edges and stayed behind in camp during the later practice parades. Unfortunately, I also missed the great Republic Day parade! However, I did get my picture in The Statesman newspaper, pretending to play the wretched clarinet, as the youngest cadet in the camp. I only saw this picture when I was in my twenties and worked for The Statesman in Calcutta and looked it up in their archives.

One of the highlights of the trip for us was a visit to Rashtrapathi Bhavan, the palace of the President of India, a beautiful Lutyens designed building in reddish sandstone. The President, Rajendra Prasad, had laid on a reception for those who participated in the Republic Day parade. He came round and we were introduced to him—a wonderful, gracious old man (my father had met Nehru, the Prime Minister, some years earlier). We explored as much of the place as we were allowed to, but the thing that most fascinated us was the ornamental orange trees complete with small glowing fruit around an ornamental pool in a central courtyard. By the time we left they had, despite the scrutiny of the President's Bodyguard, lost about half their oranges, which we secreted in our berets, intending to eat them later. They were disappointingly bitter and totally inedible.

I returned to Madras and a day later was put on a train to travel on my own to Bangalore, still hobbling, to join the family. My father had, by then, left for Calcutta where he had secured a job. My mother, who collected me at the station on a bicycle, explained within minutes of our meeting that my brother John and I were being sent to boarding school at Montfort, Yercaud, Wensley's old alma mater, while she and my father sorted themselves out. This was a shock. How had we gone from the 'big house' in Coimbatore and then the big house in Madras to this? Our lives were taking an unwanted twist. I remember little of the month in Bangalore, where we were lodging with my mother's sister Joan and her husband, Ronnie, other than getting together the long list of items we were required to turn up at boarding school with—which included 'drawers, cotton, blue' for bathing in. Wensley, 17 years old at the time, was working temporarily at the Bangalore Brewery, producers of Kingfisher (and later Cobra) beer, free bottles of which he brought home each evening and drank as ostentatiously as would any teenager pretending to be grown up. He was far from happy that he had had to leave Loyola College to earn his living temporarily. He became even more concerned when my parents left their crates of furniture and luggage behind for him to bring up to Calcutta in due course. The journey was not easy, and involved changing trains at Madras. It was a nightmare for him and to this day he does not know how he did it.

7
The Prison Camp

In early March, Wensley took John and me up to Montfort, first by train to Salem and then a long and nauseating bus journey up the hairpin bend-riddled Shevaroy Hills to Yercaud. We had effectively been dumped. John couldn't handle Wensley's departure at the end of that first day (he was only nine years old and it was his first experience of being away from home) and chased the bus for some distance, crying piteously at being left behind. He never quite got used to boarding school and felt the cold in the hill climate and was somewhat depressed most of the time. It wasn't a good time for either of us, having gone through so much change in our young lives in such a short period.

Yercaud was a beautiful, if remote place in the Shevaroy Hills. There was a small village, an Anglican church on a hillside, but the place was dominated by two schools—Montfort for boys, (Motto: Virtue and Labour) a Roman Catholic school run by the Brothers of St. Gabriel, a French Order, and, on a hill opposite, the Sacred Heart Convent for girls—acronym SHY, which the girls weren't. The surrounding hills were covered in coffee plantations, pear and orange orchards or jungle. The two schools only met on speech days and under close supervision and total segregation—yet romances flourished, mostly conducted through the surreptitious passing of notes.

After the free, if Spartan, regime of St George's, Montfort was a shock—it was more like being in prison. A boy's day was heavily regimented and there was little free time. We awoke in the cold, dark mornings to the handclap of the Brother who supervised the dormitory. You had to get up immediately and kneel on the bare floorboards while he recited the rosary—it didn't matter what religion you were. Any boy still asleep had his bed upended with him in it—a task the Brother did without interrupting his stream of prayer. We took bets on how many thuds we would hear during the rosary.

After a wash, in cold water naturally, in a freezing shed open to the elements, the Catholic boys went to Mass and the rest to prep. This was often supervised by the feared 'Tiger' Nat Terry, a large black American ex-serviceman and boxing champion who taught boxing and—wait for it—tap-dancing—his Dancing Terrytoons were a highlight of the annual concert. Talking in prep was punished by some of the more sadistic Brothers who required you to kneel on the floor with arms outstretched sideways—a taste of the cane followed if aching arms drooped. As a special refinement, boys could be made to fetch a handful of gravel from outside on which to kneel. This was regarded then as 'character building'.

The only really free time we had was when we played sport after school—football, hockey or cricket, depending on the season, representing our house—Montfort, St Gabriel or St Patrick—I was in the latter. My footballing skills improved after I acquired a second-hand pair of football boots with somewhat upturned toes packed with what suspiciously felt like cocoanut shells. These enabled me to produce thunderous kicks, not necessarily in the right direction, and terrified the shins of the defenders. After games, you've guessed it, more prep, then dinner, then bed.

Food was appalling. It is a peculiarity of Indian Roman Catholic schools that they operated a two-tier system for food. Parents could pay more to ensure their children ate better food than the others; these kids were known as 'parlour boarders' and had a separate dining room hence, I suppose the name 'parlour'. There was a school tuck shop which served basic snacks—including, strangely, tins of powdered egg and bully beef which were wartime surplus—WWII had ended 12 years before but, fortunately for the Brothers, the concept of the 'sell by date' had yet to emerge. The tuck shop operated, like everything else in school, on a system of tokens as all money was removed and converted into plastic tokens to prevent the boys buying goods from the bazaar, especially cigarettes. You could convert saved tokens at the end of the year back into cash before going home. Needless to say the boys got parents to enclose currency notes in gifts and letters so there was a strong cash economy in existence. John and I got five Rupees a month pocket money, unfortunately sent by money order, so we got the equivalent in tokens instead.

The school had a half day off on Wednesdays—the afternoon was spent in the cadet corps. In the evening we had a film, shown in the auditorium after dinner. As Wednesday dinner was usually a disgusting mince, this was carefully saved in pages torn from exercise books for throwing at other boys when the lights went down for the film. To make up for these Wednesday afternoons off we had school on Saturday mornings—the afternoons we spent in scouts; there was a whole scout headquarters built under the church in what would ordinarily have been the crypt. We had some time off on Sunday mornings after church—when walks outside the school, or games, would be organised. The afternoons were spent in prep for letter-writing home.

I became very friendly with a tubby boy called Edwin, who I had known briefly in Stanes School. We were both new to Montfort and I suppose we stuck together for a while because we didn't know anyone else—there was little we had in common. He was bright, not very good at games and sports, preferring books to sport and had a slightly anarchic and pompous manner—bitchy, really—offering opinions and pontificating sarcastically on everything, which I found endlessly amusing. As hungry schoolboys, we were always on the lookout for things to eat and one day came by a load of jackfruit seeds which someone had discarded. We promptly built a fire and roasted the seeds in the ashes before eating them—they were delicious. Edwin, however, refused to touch them on the grounds that he did not know how they had got there and wasn't prepared to risk it, a somewhat alien concept to us boys. "You are all savages! Savages!" This was his favourite expression. "Don't blame me if you all get sick—and die horribly like pi-dogs." The irony of it all was that Edwin, alone among the rest of us, always looked well fed—portly one would say—on the school's meagre diet!

We were so hungry and fed up at the lack of variety in our food that some of us, me included, persuaded the Brother who ran the dispensary to prescribe us a tonic in the form of jars of a jam-like substance, whose name I have now forgotten. We were only interested in the jam taste—not the tonic properties. Strangely enough, the Brother never questioned why a significant number of boys were requesting this tonic. At the end of the main dining hall there was a very large cupboard in which boys could keep their personal pickles and chutneys—but by far the most common commodity there was the tonic. One day at lunch we were treated to a spectacular crash accompanied by the sound of breaking glass as an over-eager boy tried to reach something on the top shelf and brought the cupboard down.

The school attracted pupils from Iraq, Burma and Thailand who had come to improve their English. These boys were usually much older and bigger than the rest of us, which gave the school considerable advantage in sports or boxing competitions against other schools. The Iraqis tended to keep to themselves, mostly because their English was still very much a work in progress.

Every summer we went to Scouts Camp, this was an event so eagerly looked forward to that few boys went home for the short summer holidays. A few weekends before, parties of the bigger boys would go into the jungle-covered hills and clear areas in which to pitch each scout patrol's tent. These areas were usually about 800 yards apart in thick forest and totally hidden from each other. The boys in each patrol had been saving money all year to purchase a tin trunk full of goodies to take to camp to augment the basic food from the camp kitchens—condensed milk (a favourite), tinned meats, tinned fruit, cakes, biscuits, jam and tinned Kraft cheese.

We scouts turned up on Day 1 and dug latrines and constructed beds on raised platforms in the tents (to keep snakes off) hacking the wood from the trees that surrounded us with axes or billhooks. Washing was done in Aeroplane Stream, which ran at the bottom of the hill with rocky ice cold pools in which to swim. We had a nightly camp fire and sing-song, with everyone picking their way back through the jungle by torchlight or kerosene lamp to lie in bed yarning and listening to the howling of the jackals and other jungle sounds. The amount of routine was negligible—confined to bugle calls to wake you up and to announce mealtimes (you sent your representative to fetch the curry, rice and dhal for the patrol, which we then augmented with our store of goodies) and to announce the start of the campfire. We had to post sentries before going to the campfire as the local natives, known as Boyans, were known to pilfer from the tents. Being a sentry was a scary job in a pitch dark jungle and many's the time that the campfire was disrupted by a scream of "Boyaaaaaans" from a jumpy sentry, to which we responded enthusiastically and en mass in a welter of boys waving knives and other lethal weapons, hoping that just this once it was a real alert and not the product of someone's jangled nerves.

We competed to make the best totem pole and patrols sought to outdo each other in the ingenuity of their campsite. I built an entire dining room, including the table, benches and sideboard for our patrol, Fox Patrol, out of branches and saplings. The camp was real 'back to nature' stuff and hordes of young boys swaggered along in the hills in ex-Australian army bush hats (part of the scout uniform and no doubt another cheap army surplus acquisition by the Brothers) with murderous scout knives tucked into belts. No rules, no Brothers grim—and best of all, no routine. Most of us learned more about life in those two weeks than we did over the rest of the prep-filled year.

And once a year we went to NCC camp where we joined cadets from other schools. Being in the NCC was not a lot of fun as we spent too much time in marching up and down pointlessly. But the camp was another matter. We were put into rows of tents and it brought out the worst in us as we spent the entire camp sabotaging the other schools' cadets. Tent ropes were cut in the night, planks over the field latrines were sawn through and weakened, pitching the unwary into the *kakka*. The worst offenders were the Iraqi boys, larger than the rest, and extremely high spirited. Their khaki uniforms somehow never looked right on them—it would be small things, a cap worn at an angle that suggested Norman Wisdom, or a couple of buttons undone on a shirt exposing more chest than was acceptable, sometimes just sheer untidiness. I suspected that they almost courted reprimand because that gave them the excuse that night to sabotage whoever had issued the reprimand. Of course when it came to the camp boxing competition they were the undisputed champs—though they were also dangerous on the shooting range, where we fired .303 Enfield rifles, as they would take surreptitious pot shots at targets other than their own.

As a non-Catholic, I was allowed, with a bunch of the other Anglican boys, to leave the school grounds on Sunday to attend our church across the hill. We went unsupervised, which meant that we soon developed a rota whereby some went to church, the others to the bazaar or to the orchards to pilfer pears, or to the plantations to cut coffee branches to turn into walking sticks to sell to the poor Catholics to take home to Dad at the end of the year. The Anglican priest, and his congregation of elderly European planters and their wives, knew what went on but turned a blind eye to it—so long as we left a few boys to attend and one good strong boy to pump the bellows of the ancient organ. The pears and sticks were valuable commodities, but most valuable were the cigarettes we brought back from the bazaar for the older boys in school—who were required to give us the cash and a very generous fee. I did try smoking but didn't take to it—mostly because my parents were heavy smokers and I had come to dislike the smell of cigarette smoke.

The walking sticks were a cottage industry. Coffee was introduced to India in the 17th century, two hundred years before tea arrived. It was, so the story goes, brought by an Arab called Haarat Shahi Janab Allah Mogatabi who had with him coffee seeds that he had brought with him from his pilgrimage to Mecca. These were sown in the hills of what is now Karnataka. Coffee branches grow very straight—they produce perfumed white flowers which grow into red berries—and are ideal for making walking sticks. We stripped the bark off them, dried them, and applied brown boot polish to give them colour. To this we added a mottled effect of black dots by blowing a glass tube (pinched from the lab) through a candle or Bunsen burner flame. To finish off, a metal tip was added, usually cut from a cigarette tin. A little carving could be made round the handle to improve the looks—and the price.

My brother, John, continued to be very homesick and unhappy at Montfort. It must have been a nightmare for him, far from home and the only member of his family around was a brother he didn't particularly like. He practically lived in a blazer, originally green, but dyed black by our parsimonious parents to meet school requirements and I can still see him in it, hunched up against the cold and looking miserable. This blazer deteriorated month by month as the pockets gradually came unpicked and the buttons fell off. John continued to suffer with his nightmares which made him scream in his sleep. The first night in school, in a dormitory full of tearful junior boys, he did his thing and the whole place was in uproar. The terrified small boys feared the worst as they had been fed tales by the older boys of jackals snatching children in the night. I gather that John slept through it all.

Feast days of the major saints—particularly St. Gabriel, our Patron—were occasions for a school holiday and special lunch was laid on. Invariably, this was pork vindaloo and yellow rice. Given the times, the pork had to be freshly killed. One of the school's pigs was led into the shower block, which was a tennis court-sized place, sunk about a foot deep, with about twenty showers spaced above it (which helped to dispose of the blood). The pig was executed by the priest, who was a 'Father' rather than a 'Brother', and a notoriously poor shot, even with a shotgun at close range. We knew lunch would be on its way when, in due course, we heard a succession of loud bangs.

Using the showers for their real function was a weekly ritual that we sort of looked forward to but yet again didn't. The boys from the dormitory, all clad shivering in their 'drawers, cotton, blue', would cluster in groups under each shower head. The water would be turned on and flowed ice cold for a minute or two, gradually getting warmer until it was too hot for comfort. Then it gradually went cold again. You had to time it just right, getting the soap on and then barging the other boys out of the way to get under the water to rinse before it became uncomfortably hot or cold.

Come the end of the school year in early December we got ready to go home for a three month holiday—winter in the hills would have been unbearable in unheated dormitories. The wheeling and dealing in souvenirs came to a climax and we Anglicans redeemed the tokens we had accumulated from our walking stick trade for considerable amounts of cash. Everyone looked forward to the trip down the hills to Salem and the rail journey home. John and I had arrived from Bangalore, but we were headed home for Calcutta, over a thousand miles away, and my parents in St Thomas' School, Kidderpore. We had no idea what to expect—which was probably just as well.

Eric Thorpe and his brothers, Leonard, Owen and Richard.
Eric, my father, is on the left

Owen, Wensley, John and Susan Thorpe. Coimbatore 1955.
Owen is on the left.

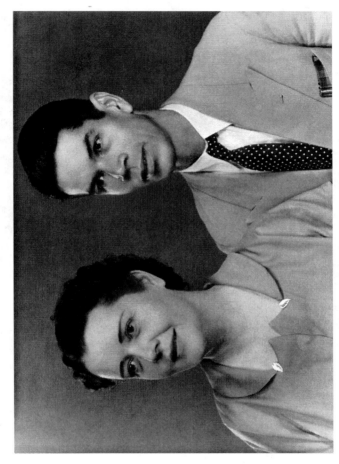

My parents, Marjorie and Eric. Coimbatore 1955.

My wedding, December 1968, cutting the cake.

Paddy and Owen out for the evening in Calcutta.
I am trying on a moustache for size! 1969

The Fathoms. A publicity picture for performances
at the Grand Hotel, Calcutta. 1963/4.

Mike, Man and Owen—my short-lived jazz/rock band. Mike is out of shot.

8

A Round Trip To Delhi

The journey into town from Calcutta's teeming Howrah station over the coffee-coloured Hoogly River was an exciting eye-opener. We were small town hicks who had only had a brief taste of the city when we lived in Madras. But Calcutta was in a completely different league. We goggled at the large buildings and impressive historical monuments to the Raj, and we had never before seen people, buses, trams, taxis, rickshaws, bullock carts, bicycles and beggars jostling so frantically and noisily for space in the streets. However, this excitement was tempered by our surprise and disappointment at the poor accommodation in which my parents lived. A small corner of the ground floor of St Thomas' Boys School (Motto: Except the Lord build the house, they labour but in vain that build it) had been separated off with a crude plywood partition and door. There were two rooms and a bathroom. One very large room functioned as a bedroom for my parents and sister. The other long, narrow room was divided in two—the first part was a small kitchenette with a kerosene stove and a bed for Wensley, in the second half, partitioned by a curtain, John and I were to sleep. As there were no proper cooking facilities, meals were delivered to us at lunch and dinner time in 'tiffin'[1] carriers. My parents, being short of cash, only ordered four meals, but there were six of us. It left us perpetually hungry, and thin, and I can remember a blazing row between Wensley and my parents over who had eaten half a piece of fruit! We had no servants and it was a real comedown from what we were used to.

Inexplicably, we also shared this cramped 'flat' with a dog called Sugar, a Silky Sidney, who was friendly and, critically, small. I could see that John and I would be on our way back to boarding school unless my parents' fortunes improved.

---

1   Tiffin means luncheon. 'Taking tiffin' was a term popularised under the Raj. The delivery of meals by tiffin carrier is a hugely efficient operation and is big business in the major Indian cities.

My parents' first task on our return was to separate John's feet from the Wellington boots he had worn throughout the three day journey from Montfort, not ever taking them off, even to go to bed. When the boots came off the smell was indescribable and it was days before they successfully got the embedded muck off his feet. The boots went to a well-deserved and no doubt pungent funeral pyre.

Children are very adaptable and before long, and it being Christmastime, we had made lots of friends with the children of the other teachers and I had acquired my first girlfriend, Valerie, the daughter of one of the teachers. She was a bubbly tom-boy who was slightly older than me.

I spent many hours with friends in the 'jungle,' a wooded area at the end of the Girls' School playing field, much used by the boys and girls for their amorous trysts—though we, in our innocence, were climbing the trees. The entry to the Boys' School was through a green door and girls waiting to see their boyfriends would hang around behind the green door.

John and I were enrolled in the school—I was now in the Ninth Standard. We didn't seem to do much study, certainly not compared to Montfort, and the atmosphere was very easy going. Having girls in my class again for certain lessons, and sassy teenage girls too, was something of a new experience. They were very self-aware and numerous romances flourished with the gangly boys.

Wensley became friendly with a couple of the other teachers' sons and they made and flew model aircraft together. We also met his girlfriend, Rosalind, a pupil of the Girls' School who was doing her secretarial course and living in school promises—she later moved to the YWCA Hostel in the centre of the city, which was the residence for many young Anglo-Indian women who had just started out as secretaries.

Our stay in Calcutta was, mercifully, short-lived. Within months of our arrival, my father was offered the post of Headmaster of a new school being built in Delhi by the Anglo-Indian leader and MP, Frank Anthony, who had been impressed by Dad when he had met him at some conference or other years earlier—and of course he had stayed with us in Coimbatore. So we duly packed up again—we seemed to have far fewer possessions to pack with each move—and a few months later left on a train—the luxury air-conditioned Rajdhani Express—for Delhi and the Frank Anthony Public School (Motto: Courage is Destiny[1]) at Lajpat Nagar on its outskirts. This school was intended to be the flagship for a series of Frank Anthony Anglo-Indian Schools around the country.

---

[1] I've never figured out what this actually means.

The 'school' had been up and running for a year, but no habitable buildings existed and classes were conducted in tents while construction took place on the main building. We lived in the top half of a rented house in nearby Defence Colony—so named because priority was given to selling the building plots to officers from the armed services. We also acquired servants again; a cook and a young 'bearer', a teenager called Sunny. Sunny was a smart, slightly supercilious chap, but his tenure only lasted a few weeks. He was fired when my mother came home unexpectedly and found him dressed up in my father's tuxedo and bow tie, preening in front of the mirror. He had apparently been experimenting with the whole wardrobe.

One of our first social engagements was to go to dinner with Frank Anthony and his wife, Olive, at their luxurious flat in Delhi. They were very kind and hospitable and I found Frank Anthony to be very focused on his job as Leader of the Anglo-Indian Community—he was one of the two Members of Parliament assigned to the community under India's Constitution—and much of his talk, when it was not about the school, was about Anglo-Indian affairs. He was tall and impressive with greying hair, every inch the barrister that he was. My father and he got on very well and he was keen to give Dad as free a hand as possible to get the school on a sound footing. In 1969, Frank Anthony wrote a book called, 'Britain's Betrayal in India: the story of the Anglo-Indian Community', published by Allied Publishers, Bombay 1969. This is now out of print but a copy is in the British Library in London. Someone should revive it.

We moved into a flat in the school basement about six months later. This was quite a large flat as it was really designed as a series of classrooms with a communal toilet attached. Our bathroom had the luxury of two cubicles with WCs. The smell of damp cement was a constant background as work on the school building progressed and scores of labourers worked on the upper floors. These labourers lived in an encampment of temporary huts the other side of a *nullah*[1] from the school. If you looked out of the window early in the morning, or late in the evening, you would be met by the sight of a row of bare bums squatting companionably and doing their business into the *nullah*.

We acquired a new cook, who was the spitting image of the President of India, Rajendra Prasad, an ayah and a sweeper. Because of the distances involved in getting to the shops, the cook was provided with a bicycle. He was far from impressed as he was a cook of infinite superiority, having worked for the best European houses (so he

---

1   large drainage ditch

said) and this was a lady's bicycle. My mother disliked the cook's superior attitude and entered into daily battle with him when he gave the accounts of his shopping—we children usually quit the house at this point as they argued over pice[1]. He would declare in exasperation, eyes rolling, as she challenged his prices, "But Madam, wejtables is so suspensive!" I rather liked the old boy, and he made a superb drink called mango fool—green mangoes boiled with milk and sugar, then strained over ice. The thought of it makes me salivate!

The school was surrounded by open fields, some cultivated with vegetables, mainly white radish, and there were a number of old, domed Mughal tombs dotted about the landscape. The one in front of the school had a resident sadhu. As this was a new school, the most senior class was Class 9 (there are 11 Classes or Standards in an Indian school) and it was expected to be the first to progress towards the Senior Cambridge exams. I was in this class. The school set up a House system with three houses: Gidney (after Sir Henry Gidney, a former leader of the Anglo-Indians); Barrow (after Albert Barrow, a school governor who was the other Anglo-Indian MP) and Rangers (after the Calcutta Rangers Club, the Anglo-Indian social club that provided charitable help to many

---

[1] part of an Anna, so of very little value.

poor Anglo-Indians). I found myself head of Rangers House and a Senior Prefect, without any obvious talents to recommend me for either job.

Delhi is very hot in summer. There are frequent dust storms, fanned by a hot wind, 'the loo', blowing from the Thar Desert. From time to time this was accompanied by swarms of locusts that descended on the fields and plants to strip them bare. The poor farmers went frantic trying to thrash them to death with brooms before they did too much damage to the crops. Strangely enough, they never ever ate the grassy cricket field. In winter Delhi is very cold and we switched school uniform of grey cotton shorts or long trousers and white shirts to royal blue caps and woollen blazers or blue jumpers and grey trousers. We had to wear a school tie. Our school day started early and finished at lunchtime, primarily because of the summer heat, but it suited everyone to keep the same hours in winter.

My close friends were two local boys, Khandelwal and Kochar, who were in my class and took me everywhere on the crossbar of their bikes—I was forbidden the use of the cook's bike, nor would I have wanted to ride a 'lady's bike'. There was the whole of Delhi to explore. We often went to the ruined Tuglaqabad Fort and explored the dark underground rooms with their colonies of bats squeaking anxiously as they clung to the crumbling ceilings. We cycled to the Qutb Minar tower, Delhi's oldest monument, dating from the 1190s, which celebrates the triumphal arrival of Islam in India. It stands 73 meters high and we used to climb the 379 steps to the top for the glorious views—you can't do that anymore as they've closed it because of the suicides. In its grounds is the black Iron Pillar, which never rusts because it was anointed so often in the past with ghee. It dates from the 4th Century and was originally part of a temple to the Hindu god Vishnu. Visitors to the pillar stand with their backs pressed against it and try to make their hands meet behind them. I was the only one of my friends able to do this and it apparently guarantees me long life or greatness or some thing. It probably just proves that I had the most gangly arms.

We often visited India Gate, the magnificent arch that is both war memorial and symbol of freedom, standing at the bottom of the hill and facing the President's Palace, Rashtrapathi Bhavan, whose oranges I had nicked not that long ago. We often strolled down Rajpath, the grand and broad processional road which connected the two and down which I had failed to march a couple of years ago. I did, the next year, get to see the full Republic Day parade as a spectator, and stood there thinking wistfully that I had missed a great opportunity to be part of the magnificent pageant of soldiers and cavalry marching past in their colourful turbans and tunics, some regiments with kukris drawn, others with camels and mules bearing mountain guns—and I saw my old school band march past too, headed by the wonderful Fritchley. Our main reason for visiting the India Gate area was to hire the rowing boats on the artificial lakes that lined Rajpath, the money for which we had pestered our parents. We raced each other up and down the long lakes for hours on end.

We also loved the magnificent setting, surrounded by the red sandstone architecture of Sir Edwin Lutyens, who was commissioned by the Raj in the early 1900s to design the main government and legislative buildings in New Delhi to reflect its Imperial status, and to lay out the well ordered gardens. Lutyens produced some memorable buildings but also made some mistakes. He miscalculated the gradient of the hill on which the President's Palace stands so that it is not entirely visible from the base of the processional route on Rajpath. He also took no account of the number of servants that would be required to maintain the 340 rooms of the Palace and its 340 acres of grounds. Under Lord Mountbatten, the last Viceroy of India, the Palace employed 400 gardeners including 50 bird-chasers! The staff problems clearly continued in my day as there were not enough garden staff to prevent the President's oranges being nicked!

We also haunted the bazaars of Old Delhi, especially the one near Chandni Chowk, the main shopping street, where you could pick up a variety of war time surplus stuff cheaply—if only the Brothers grim had known! We had ambitions to make a film using old gun cameras from aircraft—of course it never materialised. I also tried my hand at building an X-Ray machine—a coil of wire in a glass tube from which we had drawn out the air to try to create a vacuum—again a hopeless failure. I did write about one of our adventures, sending up rockets fuelled by soda-bicarb, which was published in The Statesman newspaper's Benji League page—for which I received 8 Rupees. The Benji League was a sort of children's club, named after Benji, a fictional mongoose. I still have my membership card and can do the secret sign:

'The hands are folded and raised to chin level, when the first fingers are placed under the chin, while the other fingers, folded together are to the front. Do the sign quickly—never stay in that position.'

As if! It was run by a character called Uncle Jack, who I finally met when I joined the newspaper. His real name was Reginald Maher, a good journalist and a well known Anglo-Indian author[1].

Like many young boys at the time, we were experts in using catapults, often for target practice, but sometimes to try to kill birds for sport. I had few qualms about do-

---

[1] He wrote a book called 'These are the Anglo-Indians.' Swallow Press, Calcutta 1962.

ing this. One day, one of my friends acquired an airgun and we set out that evening to hunt the pigeons that occupied the old Mughal tombs. I have always been a fairly good shot, having had lots of practice in the past, and on this occasion brought down a pigeon sitting on the roof of one of the tombs. As I went to inspect it, drops of blood began to ooze from the wound in its chest and it opened its eyes briefly to look at me before it died. That was it. It had such a profound effect on me that I never shot another bird ever again (though in England I did pot a mouse that poked its head out of a gap in the skirting—we were having a vermin problem and it was a good snap shot with an air pistol).

My other close friends were two girls in my class—Joan and Geraldine. Joan's father was a school Governor and Geraldine's mother was a teacher. We spent a lot of time together during the day in class and during the breaks, and often in the evenings when the teachers and Governors got together in school for meetings and they came over with their parents. Joan was fun and very sensible—eminently likeable. Geraldine was pretty and sporty and before too long, she became my girlfriend but, given her popularity, she proved too hard to hold on to.

Khandel and Kochar also introduced me to the riotous festival of Holi, which is celebrated with great gusto in the springtime up North. During this time it is advisable to wear your oldest clothes as groups roamed the streets spraying coloured water or throwing coloured powder on anyone passing by—irrespective of class or caste. We joined in too. Some groups threw paint, which was unpleasant, but the worst was to daub someone with used motor oil, which left them smelly, black and greasy, and had a sting in the tail because when washed off it left a yellow stain on the skin which took weeks to get out. It was probably toxic too.

Around this time, television was being introduced into India. The sets were very expensive and the service, which was in Hindi, only ran for about three hours each evening. Next door to the school was a local community centre that had a set, which they wheeled out every evening onto their front lawn so people could sit around in the cool of the dusk and watch the news and documentaries. It was all in black and white. We children were not impressed as it seemed very inferior to films. Needless to say, this set was on at full volume.[1]

There was great excitement when Queen Elizabeth II visited Delhi in 1960 while we were there. My parents, being British citizens, were invited to a garden party at the British High Commission, and excitedly recognised

---

[1] TV didn't really take off in India until the late 1970s. Up to 1977 fewer than 700,000 TV sets had been sold in a country of nearly a billion people.

themselves in a picture of the crowd in the next day's Statesman newspaper—my mother wearing an unaccustomed hat. They gave me one of their tickets to see the Queen making a speech on the Delhi *maidan*. For me it was knock-about stuff as the Queen mispronounced every Indian name—for example, Durgapore, pronounced 'Doorgapoor' became 'Durger (rhymes with burger) paw'. The British still do it today, unable to say 'Parkistharn'— as it is correctly pronounced—but insist on calling it 'Packistan'.

A short digression into language here: relatively few Anglo-Indians became really proficient in Indian languages, which of course hampered their attempts to find jobs and integrate into Indian society later in life. India has scores of languages and dialects, the main ones spoken were Hindi, Urdu and Punjabi in the North of India, Tamil and Malayalam in the South, Maharashtrian and Gujarati in the West and, of course, Bengali in Bengal. Anglo-Indian speech and its inflexions were influenced by the local languages and local words and phrases inevitably crept into the Anglo-Indian vocabulary.

Someone described Tamil as sounding like rattling marbles in a tin—so of course Anglo-Indians in the South of India spoke rapidly and rolled their 'Rs' and wobbled their heads from side to side in the Tamil way. Because Indian languages place equal stress on every syllable in a word ('I'm go-ing, are you come-ing'), we tended to do so too in our spoken English—but up to a point. English usage was also coloured by colonial Raj speech, which drew from the more upper class English accents. Recently, a colleague at work in London was amused because I pronounced 'flower' as 'flaar' rather than the current London Estuary equivalent, 'floww-wer'. I also pronounce 'hospital' and 'Martin' without a hard sounding letter T.

Playground rhymes were cobbled together from a mixture of Indian and English words: 'Inty minty papa tinty, tarn toon tussa', ugly buggly boo, out goes you' was the formula for choosing sides for games in Bengal, but not in the South. The South tended to use 'Hic, hac, hoc', fluttering our hands and on 'Hoc' placing them palm up or down—all of those with palms down, say, would become one team. There were silly playground chants like, 'Fatty fatty bomba latty, ate up all the ghee chapatti' used to cruelly taunt pupils who were overweight. Children were lulled to bed with the song, 'Ninni baba ninni, makhan, roti chini¹'.

Of course the defining characteristic of Anglo-Indian speech is the use of the word 'men' at the end of sentences, sometimes pronounced 'min'. As in, "Are you coming to

---

1   Sleep baby sleep, butter, bread and sugar. It does suffer in translation!

the pictures, men (min)?" The origin of this is attributed to the Welsh 'mun', still a common feature of some Welsh speech, and the Anglo-Indians have inherited the Welsh sing-song inflection. An Air India advertisement in the 60s featured a beautiful Anglo-Indian 'Air Hostess' (a job description now, sadly, in these politically correct days called 'cabin crew') with the caption: 'She was a Dum Dum[1] blonde. To her Calcutta was Cal, Darjeeling was Darj and men to her were something that only came at the end of her sentences.' It is interesting that the West Coast Hippies used 'man' a lot in their speech, which has become more widely used in both America and the UK, and folks in the Caribbean say 'marn'.

My father spoke a little Urdu as he was brought up in Lahore, now Pakistan. My mother spoke a little Tamil. Neither could speak the other's second tongue. When we lived in Coimbatore and Madras my mother gave the instructions to the servants, in Delhi my father did so—unless of course they spoke English. We children picked up a smattering of both Tamil and Hindi, the latter was a compulsory subject at school as it was the official language of India. I can read Hindi and speak it at an elementary level, but have forgotten most of my Tamil—though remembered enough of it to screw a

---

[1] Dum Dum is Calcutta's airport.

good price out of a Tamil trader in Malaysia not long ago. My mother forbade us the use of 'men' at the end of our sentences as she considered this a no-no. Interestingly, as she got older she used 'men' more and more in her everyday speech, though probably ironically! My wife, Paddy, and I must have sounded as though we had come out of a Peter Sellers movie when we first came to England, but our Anglo-Indian accents soon rubbed off though, thank heavens, not completely. They do become more pronounced when we are among Anglo-Indian friends.

When the English arrived in India some attempts were made to teach newcomers essential words and phrases by developing a phrasebook which constructed sound-alike English sentences. For example, "There was a cold day" was supposed to sound like "*Durwaza cole dho*" (open the door). This must have been hilarious and if anyone out there has a copy I would love to see it.

I recently got a book out of the local library, it was called Pick Up Your Parrots and Monkeys—the life of a boy soldier in India. The author gave a useful glossary of Indian terms for his European readers—but these served to indicate how the language was bastardised by the Europeans. Some examples:

buck jow go away [should be '*bagh jao*']

bunduck rifle [*bun-dhook*]

chuberao keep quiet [*chup rao*]

idderao jao ('Itherow towards me jow') come here, towards me go [doesn't make sense. '*Idderao*' means 'come here', '*jao*' means 'go']

mukkin butter [*makhan*]

puggled pawnee alcohol [*pagla parnee*—which means 'mad water'. The usual Hindi word for alcohol is '*sharab*']

tum sewer cabutch you son of a pig [*thoom soor ka batcha*]

Now back to Frank Anthony School. I represented the school in hockey and cricket—I was a reasonable left-arm spin bowler, though batted right hand. When basketball was introduced I found I was good at it because I was somewhat ambidextrous and became captain of the school team. We often took on the local urchins at cricket, played on scrubland, which we often had to clear ourselves, with tennis balls and bats made from planks of wood. These matches were taken very seriously with the full panoply of umpires and scorers.

A big annual fixture was the Founder's Day cricket match, held on the 25th September, when the boys played the teachers and school Governors. My father had attempted to create a grassy cricket pitch, like the English ones, but this was a forlorn hope in an arid climate like Delhi's. So the pre-match ritual consisted of members of the team carrying out to the pitch a green coir mat which was laid down the length of the pitch and held in place with large steel nails. This was fairly standard practice in India. My father was a good cricketer as were some of the younger teachers, and it was a close fought contest. Both teachers and boys practised in the cricket nets before the event and it was then that I discovered my father's cricketing ability. He nearly put paid to our dog, Sugar, which accompanied him everywhere, when he accidentally struck it squarely on the side of the head with a well driven ball. The dog was out cold for about five minutes before we revived it. It was somewhat accident prone, managing to fall over the edge of one of the unfenced and uncompleted upper stories of the building, damaging its back. This gave it a distinctive hump-backed shape.

One year, while bowling (slow left-handed 'leg breaks') to Mr Barrow (School Governor after whom Barrow House was named, who was one of the Anglo-Indian MPs) at the Founder's Day match, the ball shot up off a bump in the imperfect pitch and hit him on the bridge of his nose, breaking his glasses in two. Though embarrassing, it meant that he was effectively dismissed as he could not bat without his glasses. He was furious.

When your parents are also your teachers it is difficult to know how to address them in school. You can't say 'Mum' or 'Dad', and Miss or Sir sounds absurd. In the end we children simply fudged the issue and avoided addressing them in any way. I had plenty of opportunity to perfect the non-addressing issue as my father was also my maths teacher and I was not very good at maths. He was a good teacher though, and popular with both pupils and staff. My father told the story of when he tried to help one parent, who had come to enrol his children. His surname was Bagga, and my father pronounced it as it is written. "No Sir," said the parent, "it is pronounced Bugger, we have always been Buggers." His two sons were consequently known in school as Big Bugger and Little Bugger—said of course with great relish by the pupils.

The teacher who, I suppose, had the biggest effect on me was my English master, Mr Viera. He was an elderly Anglo-Indian with a toothbrush moustache and very precise, clipped speech. He encouraged me to write creatively, and gave me a sound basic foundation in English grammar and usage. I still wince when someone says 'due to' when they mean 'because of'—Mr Viera, who taught me the difference, would have winced too. The same goes when people say 'less' when they mean 'fewer'.

After school hours, I frequented the local bazaar with my friends and most of all I loved drinking a delicious milk, vermicelli and syrup drink called *faluda*. Unfortunately, one day I felt unwell enough for the doctor to be called and I was diagnosed with typhoid from the contaminated milk. I was starved for 28 days and dosed with the latest, for India, mycin drugs. Because typhoid is highly infectious, I was moved to a partitioned alcove in the hall of the flat—there was a bed and a 'thunder box'. Despite the risk of infection, my school friends used to sneak in at break times to see me. At the end of the 28 days, by now very thin and weakened, I foolishly took part in leaping over a vaulting horse and detached part of the retina in my left eye—I didn't know it at the time and told no one that my vision in that eye had turned cloudy because of the haemorrhage. Worse still, I got a relapse of typhoid and a further 28 days' starvation. I missed over two months of study for my Senior Cambridge exams. 1960 was not turning out to be a good year for me.

During the second bout of typhoid, the whole building shook one evening as an earthquake struck. There was little I could do as I was too weak to get out of bed and run, but a terrified John shot out of the building like a champagne cork from the bottle. There was no damage but, for days afterwards, my father and Wensley—who was home from teacher training college for the holidays—would panic John by simply shouting, 'Earthquake'.

The typhoid also put paid to my ambition to join the Army and apply to the National Defence Academy at Khadakvasala. My father was not keen on my going into the services, and in my weakened state I certainly would not have passed the physical. A few boys from my class did apply—my friend Khandelwal got into the Air Force but bounced a plane on landing during his pilot training and had to settle for being a navigator. Another boy got into the Army, he was later injured in the fighting between India and China. One boy, Ravi, joined the merchant navy and I met up with him in Calcutta docks years later when his ship was in port. We drank too much Scotch, with only tinned Kraft cheese to sop it up, and I fell all the way down the gangplank on my way out—with absolutely no ill effects. The hangover next morning was an altogether different matter. Another, Mukthar became a commercial pilot for Indian Airlines and was later sadly killed in a crash on the approach run to Delhi's Palam airport.

While the typhoid was doing its work on me, other machinations were taking place around my parents. Both were enthusiastically part of a heavy social scene, frequently out in the evenings at the Gidney Club in Delhi where tombola (now called Bingo) was the entertainment of choice. They drank and gossiped with a wide circle of friends. None of us children knows exactly what happened but about six months later, while I was in my final year my father was asked to resign from his job. It was said that he and a group of School Governors were planning a boardroom coup against Frank Anthony but that one of the key players lost his nerve and revealed the plot. Whatever the reason, my father's resignation put paid to him ever finding further work as a teacher in any Anglo-Indian school in India.

It was the summer of 1961. This was a huge shock to us children. Still recovering from the effects of the typhoid, I was packed off to Srinagar in Kashmir on my own by rail and bus to stay with Uncle Ronnie and Aunt Joan (my mother's younger sister) and their four year old son, Christopher. Meanwhile, my family packed up and moved back to Calcutta where my mother was given a temporary job as a teacher in St Thomas' Girls School (we had left St Thomas' Boys School two years ago!). She was allocated one room in the female teachers' quarters in which to live with Susan.

I didn't know at the time that my father had decided to leave the country and go to the UK. Wensley was coming to the end of his teacher training course in Poona, sponsored by Frank Anthony, and was expected to return to the school in Delhi to teach (which in due course he did; the Anthonys became very fond of him). John was put into St Thomas' Boys School as a boarder and I was to join him on my return from Kashmir.

I enjoyed Srinagar though there remained the nagging worry about what awaited me on my return to Calcutta. Little did I know that I would not see my father for another nine years. I was 15.

Uncle Ronnie, a jolly, easy-going, moustachioed man with a well-developed sense of humour, was a Flight Lieutenant and Navigator on transport planes in the Indian Air Force stationed in Srinagar—then a sensitive posting because of constant fears that the Chinese would mount another attack on India. Aunt Joan was thin and elegant. They were kind and very good company. We lived in a wooden house, the first I'd been in, and I cycled every afternoon up the hill to the Officers' Mess to fetch a tiffin carrier of lunch for Joan and myself. These daily trips soon brought my strength back. Shopping or entertainment in Srinagar involved crossing the river, often in the dark because night falls quickly in the tropics, in flimsy rowing boats called shikaras, which ply for hire like taxis. Srinagar is very beautiful with its many lakes, mountains and houseboats—but is sadly now too dangerous to visit because of the Indo-Pakistan dispute.

We sometimes dined with one of Ronnie's air force friends, a chap known as 'Killer'. I asked why he was so called and was told that he had flown regular patrols over the Indo-Burmese border during WWII without encountering the enemy. On one patrol he was informed over the radio that Japan had surrendered and that the war had ended—he was asked to return to base. Disappointed at not having fired his guns in anger, he allegedly chanced upon a lone individual on the road below, decided he was Japanese, and immediately strafed him to bits. I wonder…

I returned from Kashmir around July to find my mother in her one room, my father with friends and preparing to leave for England in September. I went straight into boarding school again. We were back were we had started, only our circumstances were further reduced. One minor consolation was that I knew some of the boys and teachers in the school and in my class. The big problem, as if there weren't enough already, was that I had missed three months of study because of illness, and worse still, the lessons I needed had already been covered by St Thomas' and the ones I'd done they had yet to cover. So I spent my time in furiously trying to catch up and prepare for my Senior Cambridge exams in December while also trying to come to terms with what was happening in the family.

I also, at this time, went through a significant—to me—rite of passage. Up to now I had only worn short trousers and had been getting steadily uncomfortable about doing so—I was 15 year's old for God's sake! I was growing taller but my legs refused to fill out and could have done duty as doubles for Mahatma Ghandi's spindly shanks. It didn't help that my knobbly knees were scabby from a lifetime of rough and tumble. So, despite the cost, I argued for and secured from my parents several pairs of long trousers. At last I could face impending manhood with the confidence it deserved.

My father's departure was very low key. We said goodbye to him and he went off and caught a train from Howrah Station to Bombay. From there he took a ship to Genoa and then travelled overland by rail to London. It was cheaper than flying and money was tight.

I threw myself into school life and it wasn't long before I had become a member of the choir of the very historic St John's Church—to which we choirboys trooped every Sunday by tram and then a long walk from the Esplanade—which is when we usually lost a couple of the senior boys, who disappeared into the bazaars. We also turned out for weddings and for the annual Masonic services, quite intrigued to see grown men wearing little aprons and regalia, but quite happy to attend as the Masons were generous in their payment to the choir. We had a great choirmaster, Mr Soul, who sometimes invited the boys over to his imposing air-conditioned house in Ballygunge for tea and croquet! I learned to serve as an altar boy in the school's church and had the embarrassment of having to take

Holy Communion before I was confirmed—I was the only other person present at an early morning service and when the priest advanced on me with the wafer and the wine I didn't have the heart to refuse! I also took part in amateur dramatics and I finally learned to dance, courtesy of Betty in the Girls' School who persevered with me.

It was every teenage schoolboy's ambition to learn how to dance so that he could participate more fully in the regular school 'socials' and, hopefully, get into a clinch with one of the girls at the last dance, when the lights were dimmed. We practiced in the dormitory learning the 'box step'—which most of us did mechanically and without any sense of rhythm. Learning how to jive was about as achievable as getting to the moon. We newly trained dancers would line the walls of the function room, looking shifty and trying to psyche ourselves to go over and ask a girl to dance. It took a lot of willpower to do so when we knew we were so useless at dancing, but teenage hormones provide a powerful incentive.

My Senior Cambridge results were, in consequence, very average (they were in fact better than those of my former classmates back in Delhi!). This was enough to get me on to a pre-university course at St Xavier's College, Calcutta—run by Belgian Jesuits and one of the top two colleges in Calcutta. I worked hard to do well in my pre-university exams so as to secure a place on a BA Degree course.

My mother was fortunate enough to get a permanent teaching post in Pratt Memorial School, a girl's school—mainly because the school's Principal, Mrs Bobb, was sympathetic to her plight, having met and become friendly with my parents at some School Heads' conference. We moved there at the end of the year after I had finished my Senior Cambridge exams. My mother's was the only income coming in. My father was now in the UK and Wensley was teaching in Frank Anthony School. John was found a place as a free boarder in La Martiniere School[1] and I lodged with my mother and sister Susan in one room in the female teachers' quarters at the top floor of Pratt Memorial while doing my Pre-University course. This was a temporary arrangement and I needed to secure a place in St Xavier's College hostel, but my mother couldn't afford the accommodation charges and the Jesuits were not greatly charitable as I was Anglican and the wrong denomination. We were very strapped for cash and there was no money for luxuries as my mother had three children to support. Our food came in by tif-

---

[1] A famous school founded by the French adventurer Claude Martin. The boys in the Lucknow branch of the school fought for the British in the Indian Mutiny of 1857, successfully defending the school against a series of attacks.

fin carrier as the one room in which we lodged had no real cooking facilities. My mother did, however, cook occasionally on a small kerosene stove to supplement our meagre food.

I duly applied for a scholarship from the Calcutta Rangers Club and turned up to sit the competitive exam only to find that they had got my dates mixed up and the exam had taken place a day earlier. My mother was at her wits end. Mrs Bobb exerted pressure and Rangers reluctantly relented and let me take the exam. I topped the results and they had no choice but to award me the scholarship—so I could now begin my university course in June 1962 to read politics, economics and English.

I couldn't wait to get out of the room in Pratt Memorial. The other rooms, classrooms really, in the same corridor were occupied by single female teachers and we shared communal toilet and bathing facilities. The teachers were very kind. They ranged from two young (and exceedingly beautiful) women from Kerala to a couple of middle aged Anglo-Indians and the elderly Miss Wiltshire who had managed to walk out of Burma to freedom following the Japanese invasion. Despite their kindness and tolerance, the presence of a 16 year old male was disconcerting to both parties. I also hated having to go to college in the morning through the gauntlet of the girls' school, where I was an object of curiosity. In that one room we lived, ate and I studied; there was no privacy. My father sent occasional money to my mother, wrapping the £ notes in the pages of magazines in order to circumvent the currency restrictions. My mother banked these, after exchanging them for Rupees at the more favourable black market rates. She was saving hard for the fares to leave India with her family to join my father.

She decided that it was time for me to be confirmed. I attended confirmation classes in St James' Church next door, feeling out of place as I was probably the oldest there. I had been fairly religious in an Anglican way—attending church, being in the choir, serving at altar—and I loved the Bible stories. But my faith was severely tested when the priest who ran the confirmation classes announced that the evening before the confirmation ceremony we would all have to attend confession individually. This threw us into a state of confusion—it was not the Anglican way. I mean, this left me with about 15 years' worth of sin to trot out! We kids conferred among ourselves and decided that we would adopt a general statement covering our sins, which we would each put to the priest. So I duly went before him and said, "Father I have told lies, said bad words and committed bad deeds." The blighter turned to me and said, "Go and recite The Lord's Prayer three times—and wash your private parts in cold water every night before you go to bed!" I was astonished, and from that moment on decided that I couldn't take any of this seriously. I went through the motions of being confirmed by the Bishop the next day, but I'd lost my faith.

I suppose the seeds of my atheism were planted in those nights under the stars in Coimbatore, when I started to realise that we were only a very small part of a huge universe. We are arrogant if we think that we, stuck on this little blue planet, with scant knowledge of anything outside our solar system, have identified the true creator of the universe and can plot the course for the rest of the worlds out there. It defies logic, it lacks evidence, and yet we fight wars in the name of religion.

Around this time Wensley decided to get married. Though he and Ros, his bride-to-be, were living in Delhi, they decided to get married in Calcutta where both had most of their relations and friends. The complicating factor was that the bride and groom had recently quit the Anglican Church to become Methodists, so they intended to get married in the Methodist church in Dharamtollah, even though they had never set foot in it. I was to be the Best Man.

A couple of days before the ceremony, they arrived in Calcutta, went to the church and met the priest. On the day, it was a morning wedding, we were all assembled in church awaiting the arrival of the bride. She turned up on cue, but there was no sign of either priest or organist, so she was asked to drive around the block for a further 10 minutes. The 10 minutes passed, the bride reappeared, but still no priest and organist. My mother grabbed my arm and we marched off to the vestry. There we found the priest sitting with his feet up, reading a detective novel. With one sweep of her arm, my mother yanked his feet off the desk, resisting the temptation to give him a couple of good slaps, and demanded to know, "What the hell is going on?" The startled priest protested that he thought that the service was not for another half hour and that he was waiting for the organist to start up. He was frogmarched into the church by my mother, me bringing up the rear, to await the bride.

The bride arrived, but where was the organist? So, one member of the congregation kicked off an opening hymn to accompany the bride's stroll down the aisle. All went well until we reached the chorus and then it became clear that we had started off too high and wouldn't be able to reach the notes. So we stopped. And started again, only a bit lower this time. As the ceremony progressed we got to the part where I, as Best Man, had to present the two wedding rings, and I had been instructed by Wensley that there was to be an accompanying envelope containing the priest's fee. The priest turned to me to ask for the rings and in a loud stage whisper said, "Have you brought the money?" By this time we didn't care and the congregation were giggling openly. After the ceremony we went to Pratt Memorial School for the reception. Wensley had asked one of his friends, Mike, to make the speech and propose the toast. Mike got a little carried away and declared, "Wensley! When is he? Where is he? What is he?" Well, we didn't know, or particularly care at that point.

Uncle Bob, who was now living in Calcutta, solemnly recorded it all on his cine camera—or so we thought! Unfortunately, he had set his shutter speed wrongly and the entire film was a blank except for brief flashes of the couple cutting the cake, caught in the bright lights of the camera flashes. Bob continued to present this film for inspection in the years to come, even though the actual visual content was about two seconds.

In the run up to her departure for England, my mother began to dispose of linen, crockery, cutlery and pictures she had accumulated through her married life—there simply wasn't room for it and she could not afford to ship it to England. One day she said that she had something she wished *me* to dispose of. This turned out to be a Webley and Scott .45 calibre service revolver that my father had brought back from the war in Malaya—which I never knew he had. The revolver was in a tin box in my mother's room, wrapped in a greasy rag. In India, possession of an unlicensed weapon meant a jail sentence. Just before my mother left for England I passed the weapon on to a police sergeant friend who disposed of it for me. My father had come back from Malaya with a number of trophies—a samurai sword taken off a Japanese officer, a large, ornately carved camphor wood chest, a clock from a Japanese Zero fighter plane. All of these were sold over the years along with a number of fine porcelain tea sets they had acquired—ones where the head of a Geisha was visible through the transparent porcelain at the bottom of the teacups.

I have often wondered what drove my talented father to keep landing himself in difficulty when he had every opportunity to make a good career for himself. Frank Anthony was impressed by his organisational skills and, with Anthony's patronage, he could have made a real and lasting contribution to the Anglo-Indian community. Dad was a bright, personable and very able man, well liked and with a good track record of improving the schools he was working in. My mother once said that he hated being poor as his father had died early—Dad was only 19 at the time—and the family struggled financially. As a child he stoned the carriages of the richer people out of sheer envy. His ambition to go to university was frustrated because his father died when he was in school and the family simply did not have the money to educate him further at university—though two of his brothers did go. I often wonder whether he suffered as a result of my mother's tendency to be bossy and over critical. They just seemed to pull in different directions.

9
Jesuits And Rock 'N' Roll

From a teenager's perspective, St Xavier's College, Calcutta was ideally situated—on fashionable Park Street, about 800 yards further along from the restaurants and nightclubs. St Xavier's was one of India's most prestigious colleges and attracted a mix of students from the very rich (the billionaire steel tycoon Laxmi Mittal went there, and we had boys from the Nepalese and Bhutanese royal families) to people like me on charitable scholarships. Its hostel accommodated boys in single, double and three-seater cubicles—with varying costs to match. Being a Catholic-run college, of course the infamous parlour boarder system operated. As I was on a charitable scholarship I got the most basic level of accommodation—a three-seater—and basic food (which was curry and rice and a thin dhal for both lunch and dinner).

The hostel was run by Father Leeming, a friendly Anglo-Indian Jesuit, who I was told had once represented India in hockey at the Olympics. We had a common room which had a radiogram, whose electricity was controlled from Fr Leeming's office, and a table tennis table, a piano room and a billiards room with two tables.

An alternative social centre and an essential source of emergency supplies for the hostel boys was Modi's shop across the road. The Modi brothers sold snacks, drinks and cigarettes, often gave credit when funds were low and were always friendly and helpful—my brother used to store his cycle with them when he returned late to the hostel and had to get over the wall. Generations of St Xavier's boys will remember the Modis with affection. Many's the time I have sat in Modi's shop with other boys, drinking Coca Cola and simply passing the time of day.

The front door and the perimeter gate were locked at 10 o'clock each night. This was no obstacle as boys came in over the wall and then squeezed through some conveniently loose iron bars in the windows of one of the ground floor cubicles—whose occupants became used to the nightly comings and goings. Fr Leeming had a soft spot for us Anglo-Indian boys and when we came in late, but before the 10 o'clock lockdown, having missed dinner, he would pass us the keys to the kitchen and we would polish off all the leftover food, especially that enjoyed by the parlour boarders. The presence of cockroaches scurrying away as we turned on the kitchen light didn't deter us.

In addition to the college students, the hostel also had a contingent of working men, all former college boys. We had a few from Customs & Excise, and Carl James, a quiet and somewhat remote figure—known irreverently as Saint James because of his religious leanings—who was a high flyer in Delhi Cloth Mills. Carl kept to himself but the Customs guys, known as Clary and Lobby, were very outgoing and their room was a very lively place. Clary sadly drowned, together with other Customs colleagues, in an accident on the Hoogly River when transferring from a ship they had been inspecting. One of the survivors of that accident was Gifford D'Souza, whose sister, Fitzie, later married Carl James—and, of course, I eventually married Carl's sister, Paddy. It was a small, interconnected world.

We also had Eugene Edmonds, a very good drummer and a fantastic hockey player—I think he played for either Mohun Bagan or East Bengal, the famous hockey teams. He represented India in the Tokyo Olympics and came back with a gold medal which he passed around his delighted Hostel colleagues. Eugene lived in a sort of groundsman's hut near the tennis court and was out every evening playing the drums professionally for a band in one of the local nightclubs.

The Anglo-Indian boys were a loose sort of clique but distinct from the other cliques around. We were more high spirited and a favourite sport of ours was 'ducking'. This involved creeping down the hostel corridors at dead of night with plastic bags filled with water and lobbing them over the walls of the cubicles on to the unfortunates asleep on the other side. A more heavyweight variant was to lob over 'crap tins' full of water—these were cut-down vegetable oil tins which were intended for ablutions after using the toilet, instead of toilet paper—as is the Indian way, where the use of toilet paper is regarded as unclean. Ducking was, of course, infantile, but it was great fun too—unless you were the duckee!

Life as a college boy was supposed to be different—a rite of passage—with new freedoms. I think most of us arrived at college pretty immature and to some degree we continued to be treated like schoolboys rather than young adults—I was only 16 years old after all—and there were many petty rules. We were fined for transgressions, and our lectures were like lessons at school, with reading lists thrown in to reflect our more independent status—of course we never bothered to read the listed books.

The Jesuit Fathers who ran the place were mostly Belgian, but there were small numbers of priests from other countries and some from India. The kindly Fr Huart, a Belgian, oversaw us academically—he would extract my Two Rupee fines for failing to attend lectures in the most charming way. Father Schneider, a German, taught me politics and insisted on pronouncing my surname as 'Torper'. Professor Lal, the flamboyant English professor was a wonderful teacher and I tried never to miss his lectures. The Jesuits are a wealthy order and they certainly looked after themselves. We once witnessed a regular delivery of wines, spirits and foreign food to them and in the evenings they could be heard laughing and chatting on one of the verandahs in their first floor quarters overlooking the sports field, where the clink of glasses indicated that the Holy Spirit was not their only guiding force.

The Catholic boys in the Hostel were required to attend a weekend Retreat once a year. They were forbidden to talk during this period—so of course we non-Catholics did everything we could to provoke them into breaking their silence. There was a box next to the Hostel chapel into which they could post questions during the

Retreat. There was outrage one year when one question asked, 'Can we twist again like we twisted last summer?' The priests were not amused.

    I attended college lectures every day but after a year began skipping a few as my other interests developed. From larking about singing in the piano room, we decided to put together a folk singing trio and get some money by singing in Calcutta's nightclubs and restaurants. So Errol Goves, Peter Lardner and I, joined months later by a non-St Xavier's boy, Ivan John, who played the guitar, rehearsed a number of folk songs, mainly in the bathroom of Peter's friend's house as the harmonies sounded much better in the echo! We modelled ourselves on the American folk group, the Kingston Trio (famous for the song Sloop John B), and covered their material, but added comedy actions to tell the story in the songs. This was a time when there were one or two 'do wop' groups who sang Platters or Drifters songs—we wanted to be different. Very soon, we were signed up, as The Deltas (because we were on the Hoogly delta, geddit?), with the theatrical Agent, K C Sen, who had the monopoly of the entertainment acts in Calcutta. We made our debut in Trincas, on Park Street, and half the hostel came to see us. Sen booked us to sing in the local restaurants and night clubs but we were seldom paid. We were getting a lot of work but the cash wasn't rolling in.

I also became a member of the Calcutta Light Opera Group Society (CLOGS) which put on annual operettas in the New Empire theatre, where the Calcutta Symphony Orchestra, under Bernard Jacobson, provided the musical accompaniment. CLOGS had a great social scene which I enjoyed, and I took part in two of their productions, The Merry Widow and the Desert Song. The group was run by a warm and wonderful elderly English couple, Ma and Pa Augier. Ma was motherly and bustling, always had words of encouragement and comfort. Pa, with his cherubic pink cheeks, constantly puffing on a pipe, was a great organiser. The two of them were the hub of the organisation and thought nothing of having the entire cast over to their small flat at the corner of Royd Street and Wellesley Street where we would hold impromptu parties and dance and sing into the early hours. Though CLOGS existed to put on one operetta a year, the social scene it generated continued throughout the year. Pa Augier wrote a Christmas pantomime, for which we called ourselves the CLOTS (Conglomeration of Loonies, Objectionables and Thugs) and put it on at St Thomas' Free School Street—with the proceeds going to charity as usual.

Two of the members I shared a stage with, one of whom was in college with me, went on to become famous Indian film stars: Victor Bannerjee (A Passage to

India and The Chess Players) and Amitabh Bachan, possibly the most famous Indian film star ever, with his effigy in Madame Tussauds, London. Through friends in CLOGS I joined The Amateurs, a drama group, I didn't act in their productions but was part of the stage management team. I also took part in St Xavier's College amateur dramatic productions. During one of these I fell ill before opening night and suffered the most disturbing hallucinations because of my high fever—imagining that the room around me was expanding hugely while I got smaller and smaller.

Predictably, my college work suffered—I was out nearly every night.

The Deltas were spotted in 1963 by an Englishman, Toby Severn (his stage nom de plume), who wanted to set up as a rival to K C Sen and also, I think, because he was ambitious to promote the singing career of his Anglo-Indian girlfriend, Lorraine—stage name Lorelei. He introduced us to the Beatles' music and played us tapes of the latest UK groups. We changed our name to The Fathoms (you can detect the watery theme that went through our thinking in selecting the group's names) and Toby got us gigs in the better nightclubs in the Blue Fox and the Grand Hotel, and in some of the restaurants in Park Street. We wore white shirts and black trousers, blue silk waistcoats, and small black celluloid inserts under our buttoned collars that looked like very modern bow ties. I was also encouraged to do some solo spots under the name of Kit Owen. We started to make some money and I was able to help my mother save for her fares to the UK. Toby also had a girls' group that he had trained, The Blue Orchids. As the two groups tended to do their gigs together, relationships developed and Pete started going out with one of the girls, Jennifer, I with another, Judy—her cousin, but poor Errol was unsuccessful in snaring the third, Gloria—though to all our astonishment he married her many, many years later and they live in Perth, Australia. When, once, Jennifer, who was the lead singer, fell ill, I stood in for her as, having a bass voice, I was the only one who could sing her part—an octave lower.

The Fathoms broke up as we were nearing the end of our college degree courses. By now three of us were playing guitars. Our farewell concert on the stage in St Xavier's College auditorium was memorable for Errol Goves being spectacularly electrocuted in a blue flash of light as he stepped up to the mike and his lips made contact with it. It blew the fuses and extinguished all the lights in the theatre. His only after effect was a splitting headache.

There were quite a few groups around playing Park Street. The Tornados (Mike Booth and Sam Hardy) the

Hellions (Skinny and Biddu Appiah—the latter went on to write and produce the song Everybody was Kung Fu Fighting); Neil Sen and Ricky Chadburn were both in bands. Everybody was energised by the Beatles and Rolling Stones revolution and the guys began sporting long hair and Beatle boots while the girls went for bouffant hairdos supported by gallons of hairspray and can-can petticoats. They adopted a more slimline Mary Quant look when that came in. My pride and joy was a pale blue shirt with a Nehru collar and a target painted on it, in imitation of The Who. More commonly, our group wore turtle neck sweaters (in Calcutta's heat and humidity!) and imitation leather waistcoats made of something called Rexine.

I joined another set of lads, more rough and ready, in a more edgy rock band, The Wild Ones, in which I played electric bass guitar. The driving force of this group was Rico. In appearance he was an Anglo-Indian version of Mick Jagger—skinny, loose-lipped, long hair, drainpipe trousers and outlandish shirts—and led a relaxed life as his mother had won a considerable sum of money—some said a lakh[1]—in the Madras Mail's crossword competition and he did not need to work. He was a good drummer and could turn his hand to anything. He was

---

1   a lakh is a hundred thousand Rupees—a huge sum at the time.

talented at electronics and reconditioned motorbikes as a sideline—these he bought through army surplus at Dum Dum. He made most of our musical equipment.

The other members of the group were Bobby Kenny, small, fair-haired and a good guitarist and singer (his father, Claude, drummed with the band at the Blue Fox), and Clayton Saunders our pianist who was more conventionally trained and not really into rock music. We developed a dedicated following and for a time caught the eye of a group of English girls whose fathers were captains of industry in Calcutta. I briefly went out with one of them, Penny, who was startlingly pretty and was related to the actress Deborah Kerr. One of our roadies, was so taken with these girls that he began affecting what he thought was a working class English accent, modelled on hearing the Beatles on film. Unfortunately for him it sounded as though he had a serious nasal and coughing problem, but he persisted, blissfully unaware that he was making a complete fool of himself.

The Wild Ones ran for a couple of years before we went our separate ways, regularly playing the jam sessions at the Moulin Rouge on Park Street and playing at Firpo's in the evening cabarets—where we had to do a session in the upstairs restaurant then move the equipment downstairs for our second session there. We made a considerable splash in Calcutta and also provided the soundtrack to a couple of commercials—we went to the HMV recording studios in Dum Dum to do them. I did the voice of the seal that was the symbol of Kwality ice cream (now owned by Walls). In the cartoon the seal was to be pushing an ice cream cart and I had to bawl, 'Kwaaaaaliteee!' in an Indian accent, like an ice cream wallah. We also sang a jingle for Brooke Bond Tea written by a smooth ad executive at J Walter Thompson, the advertising agency:

> *Fresh supplies in your shop every week,*
> *Its Brooke Bond tea, its flavour at its peak!*
> *Wherever you are, wherever you may be,*
> *You can rely on Brooke Bond tea.*
> *Brooke Bond tea for you, you, you and me!*

Hardly stirring stuff (no pun intended). I also had my portrait painted in full Wild Ones rig: red jacket with black piping, yellow frilled shirt, black drainpipe trousers and my signature teardrop-shaped canary yellow bass guitar, by the Statesman's Art Director—I wonder where both portrait and guitar are now. The Art Director became infamous for designing an advertisement for underarm deodorant with the slogan: 'Let your armpits be your charmpits!' This was before they let me loose on designing future campaigns.

The teardrop-shaped guitar was hand made by Rico from solid teak as we could not afford proper instruments because of the high import duty which inflated the costs. It weighed a ton. Though we had never seen a real bass guitar we worked out the proportions very ingeniously. At the time we were avid readers of Fab magazine, an English publication which carried pictures and stories of the latest pop groups in England. By knowing the height of some of the bass guitarists who were pictured with their instruments, we used art school techniques and worked out the proportions of their instruments. We went down to the timber yard, drew the outline of the guitar on a plank of teak and had it cut out. Rico then went to work on it and completed the fittings. My parents were persuaded to send me bass strings from England, which were an essential component and unavailable in India. I also had a big amplifier cabinet, formerly someone's corner Hi-fi speaker, which was so large and unwieldy that it went to gigs in its own rickshaw because it was too big to fit into our normal taxi transport. Moving it up and down the back stairs at Firpo's really tested our tempers.

The teak guitar proved useful more than once when drunks at Firpo's would try to get in on the act when we performed there in cabaret. A seemingly slight and 'accidental' nudge in the ribs with the bass had, because of its weight, the effect of a good punch and soon propelled the drunk back to his seat—even more the worse for wear.

We sang cover versions of the Beatles, the Rolling Stones but mostly the Animals because we loved rhythm and blues and I could sing a bit like Eric Burdon, their lead singer. We thought the Beatles were too 'goody-goody' and wanted to be rebels like the Stones. Rico's house thundered to the sounds of our rehearsals or to the loud music we played on his radiogram, and the house was often crowded with hangers-on which inevitably led to an impromptu party. He and his mother were very tolerant, warm-hearted and hospitable; once when I was between flats they had no hesitation in accommodating me on their living room floor for about a month. Rico also saved me from starvation that month when I foolishly left my month's salary in the inside pocket of a jacket that I gave to the dhobis to be washed. Soon after giving the garment in I realised what I had done and went to the dhobis immediately to retrieve my money. It wasn't there and they denied all knowledge of it. I was distraught. Rico decided to act and grabbed the senior dhobi by the collar and angrily threatened to bring in the police and turn the place over if the money was not returned. Miraculously, it was—someone there suddenly claimed to have spotted it among a pile of clothes.

I often went with Rico to Malik Bazaar on Lower Circular Road to get motorcycle parts or bits and pieces for amplifiers. Malik Bazaar was the centre of the trade in motor spares and it was said that you could virtually build a car from the variety of spares on offer—many of them machined in the backstreets. It was one reason why so many cars that would have been considered veteran cars in the West were kept roadworthy and used as regular commuter transport. The Statesman later exploited this by running regular vintage car rallies—which attracted numbers of foreign buyers who, cash in hand at the finish line would buy a good proportion of the entries. You had to keep your wits about you though when in Malik Bazaar; we heard tales of drivers who had parked their cars and gone in to buy a wheel or tyre only to be sold one stolen off their car minutes earlier as they sat drinking tea in the shop.

Rico stood no nonsense and was prepared to fight anyone who insulted his appearance—which, given its eccentricity to most Indians, was frequently. One day a gang of Bengali boys he had assaulted sought to get their own back and I was the unfortunate object. Walking down Park Street one Sunday evening with another member of our band, a taxi drew up behind us, two men jumped out and produced knives—we were bundled into the taxi and driven to the suburb of Ballygunge. They had 'kidnapped' us because we were associates of Rico's, and no doubt intended to give us a good beating. However, when we arrived at the destination, which was in the middle of a large park, we were met by a group of other boys with handkerchiefs concealing their faces. Several of them recognised me from St Xavier's, where they were also students, and remonstrated with the two who had bundled me into the taxi. They were very apologetic and then, strangely, began a discussion about politics with me—I was reading for a Degree in Politics. The friend with me was not so lucky and was being pushed and shoved as he, apparently, had been involved in the original fracas. We then had a second bit of good fortune as another gang suddenly hove into view through the trees and began to assault this one. My friend and I made good our escape and got back unscathed. I had hot words with Rico—it had been a scary and unpleasant experience.

Around this time, my old friend Rajan (the one who had recovered from smallpox) surfaced. He had heard through an acquaintance that I was in a rock band and decided to come and visit me in Calcutta. By then he was ostensibly working in the peanut business for his father and had persuaded the old man to let him come to Calcutta to drum up business. He turned up at one of our gigs one day and I could hardly recognise him—he was thick-set almost to the point of being overweight.

His pock-marked face was round and cheery—and he was as mad as ever.

Rajan was big into Bollywood films by then and constantly hummed his favourite film songs. He gave the appearance of being very shallow but it was all a front. He had an acute intelligence and told me that he expected to become the Peanut King of the South. He insisted on coming to our gigs because, he told me, he wanted to meet girls—but not the 'nice' ones! He flashed his money around and acquired 'friends' but also rubbed a few people up the wrong way because he could be very bumptious. If someone was irritating him he would smile in a friendly way and take their hand to shake it—then give them a bone crunching squeeze and as they writhed in agony would smilingly warn them that he would do them serious damage if they ever crossed him. None ever did, they gave him a wide berth after that. The girls found him charming, but scary and the romance he anticipated never occurred. Rajan and I would sit for hours over drinks in a restaurant chatting about the old days, he shivering his leg and breaking into odd snatches of Bollywood tunes. He behaved like royalty and the waiters treated him accordingly. We had a great three weeks together, some of it lost to me as we were so smashed at times.

At the end of it all, he went back to Coimbatore and promised to keep in touch—but never did. I found out that he subsequently married a woman who was a college lecturer—she wasn't very pretty but had a strong personality and Rajan adored her—and she him. It was not an arranged marriage. No doubt he will heave into view again in my life, unannounced and probably shouting, 'Thorpeeeeeeeee!" down the street to attract my attention.

As our college courses progressed, our thoughts turned to what we would do after we had graduated. For those doing their Batchelor of Commerce degrees, the way ahead was broadly clear—they would become accountants or apply for management traineeships. For those of us doing our Batchelor of Arts degrees the choices were more difficult. I was studying politics—but had little interest in becoming a politician, even if that was remotely possible. There were endless discussions with friends and one of them, Robin, told me that he intended to become a lawyer—in particular a barrister. Robin was very well equipped for this career; he had a booming voice, oodles of self-confidence, a theatrical manner and intimidating black spectacles. I thought that this might be a good choice of career—I had visions of being a Perry Mason figure dramatically winning court cases by producing clinching evidence at the very last minute—with my CLOGS experience I could be theatrical too. And of course I was aware that Frank Anthony, himself a barrister, had been involved in some sensational and important cases.

At Robin's suggestion I visited the Calcutta High Court to get a feel for what was involved. The court itself was the usual austere and forbidding Victorian building. Its verandahs and corridors were crowded with barristers, all dressed in black jackets and white trousers, some consulting with their clients before going into court, but most standing around touting for work. It was a shock to see so many, and more shocking still to realise that most of them were on the breadline as their emaciated bodies, tattered jackets and grimy trousers indicated. Clearly, there were many more lawyers out there than was work to go around. Stepping inside to the courts did little to improve the image of the profession. Instead of the ordered hush one sees in television courtroom dramas, all was confusion and bureaucracy in grimy surroundings with high ceiling fans just about stirring the dusty, thick and suffocating air. I talked to a couple of barristers outside the court and learned that it was a highly competitive profession in which only the lucky few succeeded. Most often they were paid to delay court proceedings rather than bring them to a conclusion. They kindly advised me to reconsider my career choice—with hindsight, probably to deter even more competition from a newcomer.

I realised then that being a lawyer was not for me, though Robin persisted in pursuing his career and is no doubt making a good living out of it.

Rod, another friend, and I decided that we would have our voices trained as we were always singing snatches of Mario Lanza songs in the showers at the Hostel and we thought it would help us to get better parts in the CLOGS operettas. We visited a singing teacher who lived in the flats above Flury's cake shop on Park Street and auditioned for her, singing our Maria Lanza songs in what we imagined to be proper tenor (Rod) and baritone voices (me). The look on her face said it all, and we were further deterred by the cost of the lessons—she might even have set the bar deliberately high to discourage us. So that ended our operatic delusions, which we confined from then on to the showers. It just goes to show, however, the sheer cheek and self-belief we had as teenagers. We felt we could do anything and were willing to give it a go.

In my last year at college, 1965, I met a man from The Statesman Newspaper, which was an old, independent English language national daily published in both Calcutta and Delhi, at a Fathoms gig and we chatted about my post-university plans. He said that there could be a vacancy in the Advertising Department, in which he worked, and suggested I apply. I did, attended an interview with the Advertising Manager, who agreed to take me on part time, a couple of half days a week, while I completed my degree (BA Honours in Politics). I was paid the princely sum of Rs.50 per month. I graduated in early1965, after frantic study to make up for all the missed lectures, and duly passed with a Second, and went to work for The Statesman full time—on a more agreeable salary. My job involved drafting and editing classified adverts and, later, designing advertising campaigns for clients.

I needed to move out of the Hostel and find a place of my own as I could not go back to living with my mother in Pratt Memorial School and, anyway, she was about to quit the country for England. Houses and apartments in Calcutta did not come cheap and landlords traded on their scarcity by demanding a payment of 'key money', called *salami*, before they would condescend to let you rent their property. This payment could run into hundreds of Rupees, which I could not afford. The other options were to become a 'paying guest' in someone's house, living in one room, or to remain in the Hostel if the Jesuit Fathers would allow me to. Fate, however, was to deal me a kind hand.

The Fathoms were playing Trincas one evening, and we had warmed up for it by consuming large quantities of gin. The set went well and a group of ex-St Xavier's boys came up and invited us to come on to the Dalhousie

Institute, where there was a dance. Off we went, and at the dance consumed even more alcohol. I realised I was well over the limit when I found myself on all fours, making for the toilets. A chap called Peter, who was both an ex-St Xavier's boy and a contemporary of my brother Wensley at Montfort, bundled me into a cab and took me back to his flat, knowing that there was no way I would be able to climb into the hostel over the wall—even standing upright would have been a problem! The next morning I was, surprisingly, free of a hangover and we got to chatting. He was looking for a flatmate to share his costs, I was looking for a flat—and had a job—so he asked if I would be interested. I was quick to accept.

My mother, brother John and sister Susan left India for the UK that July. The date was critical as it meant that they only had to pay the child's fare for Susan—she would have had to pay the full adult fare if they left after her 12th birthday in August and my mother couldn't afford that. She certainly did not have the money to pay for my passage to the UK, so I was to remain behind in Calcutta. As I now had a job, it was expected that I would be 'alright'. I put a brave face on it though I was filled with fear and apprehension at being left on my own. But in a way being left behind also suited me—even though it was very scary as I was only 18 years old. I was enjoying my work and social life and valued my independence and I had no real wish for yet another major change introduced by my parents and beyond my control. I blotted out of my mind the awful consequences that could befall me if I fell ill or lost my job and had no income. I would have been stranded.

I moved in to Peter's large flat in Park Circus, another big Anglo-Indian enclave. The flat was owned by his uncle and aunt, who lived on the floor below. The uncle enjoyed his booze and had had the steering wheel of his car loosened so that he could broadly drive in a straight line despite lurching from side to side when in his cups. He was quite proud of his ingenuity and demonstrated his steering to me. It did the trick—as he never had an accident.

I worked at The Statesman by day and my evenings were divided between gigs with the band, the opera group, the amateur dramatic group or going to parties. Looking back, I seem to have lived several separate lives. In that July another eventful thing happened—the arrival of Paddy in my life.

Peter's girlfriend was Carl 'Saint' James's sister, Barbara, known as Babs. Her 17 year old younger sister, Patsy, was coming to Calcutta to begin her university course at Loreto College—the poshest women's college in Calcutta, possibly in India (as far as the nuns were concerned, possibly the world!). The day after she arrived, the Monsoon hit, it rained very heavily and all the streets became flooded as they often did because the ancient sewage system could not cope. As neither Peter nor I could go to work, we decided to walk the half mile through the flood to see Babs and Patsy. This we did, wearing our oldest clothes and with raw sewage floating around us. I was very taken with Patsy, who was beautiful and very serious, with the most wonderful grey-green eyes, lustrous skin and her jet black hair in a pigtail. I think she hated me on sight.

All four of us went out to dinner at Trincas that night as the flood had subsided. Peter and Babs called Patsy 'Paddy' but I was told that only close family could call her that—I was clearly excluded. As the evening progressed Patsy became only slightly friendlier, but the chill descended again when, having had a beer or four, I told her that she was the girl I was going to marry—I instinctively knew that she was the one.

We didn't see much of each other for a while, then, six months later, out of the blue, I got a letter from her when she was on holiday back home in Delhi, and we began writing to each other. I have no idea why she changed her mind, but romance took hold. Peter and Babs did not seem too keen on the idea of us going out together and tried to split us up. I think their reasoning was that: a) I was not a Catholic; and b) as I was with a rock band I must lead a debauched lifestyle. Matters came to a head when I invited Paddy (as I now called her) to come one Sunday to St John's Church, where I had been a choirboy while in St Thomas' Boys School. It is the oldest Calcutta church, very grand as it was formerly the Anglican Cathedral, in its grounds is the tomb of Job Charnock, who founded Calcutta, and also a memorial to the infamous Black Hole of Calcutta. I wanted her to see a bit of Calcutta's past. Paddy happened to tell her sister, which created uproar in her family, who were staunch Catholics. Her mother was so upset that the father immediately decided to fly down from Delhi to put a stop to our romance.

I was summoned to a confrontation in Loreto College. I think Paddy's father was expecting a louche, long-haired, drug-taking pop musician. As I had just come from work at The Statesman, he was not prepared for someone in a collar and tie, behaving very reasonably. I explained that my intention in taking Paddy to church at St John's was to show her the history, not to convert her. Nevertheless, I was told to stop seeing his daughter and he threatened to take her out of college if we continued to see each other. Annoyed at being told what to do, I countered by saying that as I was earning enough to support her I would pay to ensure that she could remain in college. Paddy too was adamant that she wished to go on seeing me. As the discussion progressed, the father realised that both Paddy and I were deadly serious. More importantly, he began to form his own judgement of me. He suddenly called a halt to the meeting and asked me to walk back with him and we talked awhile standing on the corner of Flury's on Park Street.

Eric, Paddy's father, whom I came to love more dearly than my own parents, said to me that, having now had an opportunity to meet me, he had decided that he would not stand in the way of my seeing his daughter. He promised to put paid to all the concerns within the family—which he soon did. I was welcomed into the family by Paddy's brother Carl and his wife, Fitzie, and before too long had also established a good relationship with Paddy's mother and aunts.

Eric was very much a self-made man. Orphaned young, he was brought up by his sister, Inez, a truly remarkable woman who was widowed in the troubles following the Partition of India and Pakistan in 1947. Her husband was travelling by train from Peshawar to Lahore when it was ambushed and all its passengers slaughtered. The ambush took place on a river bridge and many of the bodies were thrown into the water, never to be recovered. Inez's husband was one of them. Though his life was insured, the insurance company refused to pay up as no body could be produced so Inez struggled hard to bring up her three children. She subsequently emigrated with them to England, continuing to provide help and support to their families. She died recently, aged 96 and will be sadly missed for the joy and enthusiasm she brought to life.

Eric learned printing and rose through the ranks of the Government printing presses to become the top man. He liked to give advice—very kindly, but in an extremely long-winded way. I spent many hours in his company learning from him—and even though he has been dead some 36 years I still miss him. He was interested in unconventional medicine and I went through both homeopathic treatment as well as dowsing by crystals to try to 'cure' the damage to my left retina. It was about as effective as the baldness cures he had tried.

By now I had moved to a room of my own in Wellesley Square, facing Wellesley Tank, a large, square pond used by the locals for bathing and washing their clothes. My room was in a flat owned by an elderly Anglo-Indian couple. The Congress Party of India had a political centre next door and had frequent, noisy meetings. The thing I remember most about the flat was the colony of large bandicoot rats that inhabited the garden, which they had pockmarked with their holes.

Shortly after moving I acquired a very noisy fourth-hand Royal Enfield Prince motorcycle which Paddy's little nephew, Carl Jr could hear a mile off before anybody else. He would stand stock still and say, 'Uncle Owen's coming' and sure enough I would arrive minutes later. Because of the motorbike I became a member of the Calcutta Motor Sports Club. We raced on an old airfield, wearing builders' hard hats for crash helmets, and enjoyed ourselves until one of the English drivers carelessly ran over a spectator with his racing car and the club was closed down. Mind you, I never ever passed my motorcycle driving test, so to race the bike, with only a builders' hard hat for protection, was sheer lunacy. When riding the bike for pleasure there was no question then of wearing a crash helmet—you would have looked out of place. My only concession to safety was to wear a pair of very lightly tinted sunglasses to keep the insects out of my eyes. Paddy rode pillion, sometimes in a sari with the end streaming behind her. It wasn't the most sensible thing to do as we had heard of a friend whose sari got caught in the wheels of the bike, tumbling her off and unrolling her sari. Fortunately she only suffered a few bruises and dented her dignity.

With my family gone, my only relatives in Calcutta were Uncle Bob and Aunt Dolly—she was my Great Aunt and her children, Bobby, who was wheelchair-bound and unable to speak following childhood polio, and Margaret, a sweet fair haired girl—my second cousins. Paddy and I visited the family and spent summer afternoons swimming in the cloudy communal pool on their housing estate with Margaret before being fed to the gills by Aunt Dolly. Shortly afterwards, Margaret married a fighter pilot in the Indian Air Force, Dara Chinoy, who distinguished himself after being shot down in combat during the 1965 India-Pakistan war by finding his way back to base on foot through enemy lines—for which he was decorated for his bravery. It was helpful having some family contact nearby in case I got into difficulty.

I decided to form another band which would play both jazz and rock. It was called 'Mike, Man and Owen' after the three band members. Mike Blaquiere was a good jazz guitarist, but I think he struggled to change his style over to playing rock, and Manfred Hamilton, who was our drummer, lived with his mother and sister in the flat below me; he had never played in public before. I had a replica of Paul McCartney's Hofner violin bass made and the band had moderate success for a short time, playing Firpo's, before it was clear that it wasn't progressing the way it should have been and we split up.

Another reason for the split was that I was moving on into writing for The Statesman and accepted that Paddy's family would never be very happy about my continuing to play in rock bands. I wrote articles on rock and short stories for the Junior Statesman magazine, whose Editor, Desmond Doig, was very supportive and when I left India gave me a glowing testimonial. Doig, who was already an acclaimed writer and artist, was a close friend of the royal family of Bhutan. He was also a friend of the actress Shirley McLaine, who visited The Statesman on occasion to see him—I had never seen so many freckles on anyone before.

In the months before we left India I passed the audition to become an announcer on All India Radio's western music programmes. The audition consisted of reading a list of the names of western classical music composers—which was easy for me because of my father's interest in classical music, so pronouncing 'Dvorak' and 'Mussorgsky' correctly wasn't difficult. The pay was stingy—I was given 10 Rupees per broadcast. I began working six evenings a month reading the early evening stock market reports (droning on about the prices for shellac!) and then doing the late evening western programmes—which could be anything from taped scientific lectures, to classical or rock music, with an occasional live broadcast of the popular Anglo-Indian Hawaiian-guitar band, 'Garney Nyss and the Boys'. I had been baptised in Bangalore in 1946 by a priest called Noel Nyss, who was, I understand, a relation. When it came to rock music I had a free hand to play what I liked and entertained Calcutta with the Rolling Stones and Animals. Whether anyone was actually listening, I can't say.

The radio station's equipment was old and rudimentary but I was kindly tutored in its ways by the eminent broadcaster, Pearson Surita. One evening, when I was playing a taped lecture on a large reel-to-reel tape recorder, the tape broke and, to try and save the day, I ended up pulling the rest of the tape slowly through the recorder. This must have sounded strange to the listeners as the lecturer's voice rose and fell in pitch because I couldn't keep up a constant speed. I ended the evening with an ankle high pile of discarded tape. I was also there when we had one of Calcutta's periodic Hindu-Muslim riots and had to do the broadcast with armed soldiers in the control room—to safeguard the radio station from take-over!

10

The Statesman

The city of Calcutta was a total assault on the senses. Rudyard Kipling described it as 'the many-sided, the smoky, the magnificent'. It was full to overflowing with people, and the population was constantly added to with an influx of people from East Bengal, now Bangladesh, and the poor from the villages in West Bengal, who had come to try their luck in the big city and ended up living on the pavements, often begging for a living. Everything was in decay—the crumbling stucco on the grimy buildings, cracked wooden shutters on the windows, the festoons of electrical wiring, banners and bunting that went everywhere, the walls and buildings defaced with posters for films or crudely stencilled slogans proclaiming the virtues of election candidates, the betel nut stained pavements, the battered trams, buses and taxis, plus a sprinkling of ancient cars (and these were real vintage pieces that still did the daily commuter run). Loose cows, goats and pi-dogs roamed the streets and wandered nonchalantly through the teeming traffic. All of this was overlaid with a rank, grimy pollution which tore at the nostrils and choked. And yet—for all its misery, it was a city with a magnificent heart and a vitality that grabbed and held you.

You would be woken early each morning by the deep grinding sound of the first trams and the hiss and splutter of the electricity sparking off their cables. Then would come the roar of buses and lorries transporting goods and passengers and the rattle of bullock cart wheels cracking along the tram tracks. Mix this with the insistent cawing of the crows and the growing hum of the crowds, the blaring into life of radios and loudspeakers with film and devotional songs, the tinkling of rickshaw bells tapped urgently on the shafts by the rickshaw-wallas as they jogged through the streets trying to avoid getting their wheels caught in those tram tracks—which could be a disaster as the wheel could be wrenched off and both rickshaw-wallah and passenger pitched onto the road. Then the feverish honking of horns as taxis and cars raced one another through crowded streets to get to wherever they were going. Anyone who has lived in India will have noticed the 'Horn Please' slogan on the backs of buses and lorries—and they meant it. Every journey was accompanied by the constant and urgent honking of horns.

Then there were the smells: early morning fires, raw sewage, cooking, diesel and petrol fumes, squalor and damp—this is a city built on a sodden river delta. The damp is all pervasive—it hangs in your nostrils and invades your shoes and clothes, leaving a film of mildew on them overnight, especially in the monsoon season, if you are not careful.

You can taste Calcutta too. Many of us woke to the early morning *halwa puri*—which is peculiar to Calcutta—but you could also taste the slightly acrid sooty dust that hung in the air. This is a city that, despite its dirt and squalor also produces the most exquisite sweets: the *rassogolla*, *sandesh* (a milk sweet), *rasmallai* (sweet cream) and, most memorably, sweet curds made in an earthenware *chattie* (pot). It also produces that hot, sweet, milky and spiced Indian tea, served each time in a brand new earthenware cup, which you smashed on the pavement when you had finished your drink. I was also partial to the corn, roasted at the roadside on *chulas*—a sort of bucket-like brazier—and dribbled with butter or ghee and salt; the warm nan breads with their slightly burnt bubbles; and of course the kathi kebabs.

Every morning, when you left the safe island of your home to go to work it was like diving into a human sea as you jostled with the crowds– all going somewhere, and the piteous, starving beggars grabbing out to attract your attention. You might have had to shove your way onto a crowded tram or bus, though getting a seat was rare. If you were unlucky, you could have your pocket picked and not know it until you reached your destination. However, if the pickpocket was caught in the act, all hell broke loose. The tram or bus was stopped by the enraged passengers and the culprit manhandled off and given a sound thrashing; Bengalis like to do it with their slippers as it avoids the personal contact which can contaminate someone of a higher caste while administering both pain and an insult as the shoes are regarded as unclean—they certainly would be in Calcutta.

It was a mixture of extreme contrasts. Great wealth shared the roads with wretched poverty. Captains of Industry in their polished chauffeur driven cars passed whole families, generations of them, living in the open on the pavements, exposed to the elements, soaping themselves under the roadside water pumps as they observed the Hindu ritual of daily cleanliness. Their lives must have been awful when the monsoon rains came and the streets flooded their makeshift beds and living spaces. Among the daily bustle in the streets would pass regular processions bearing the dead to the burning ghats. The deceased was usually placed on a charpoy[1] and, garlanded and with face exposed, would be carried aloft through the streets on the shoulders of jogging and chanting white-clad mourners—white is the colour of mourning in India. If the recently departed was a person of substance, there could be a colourful accompanying brass band, popularly known as 'Foo Foo bands', and they played an assorted mixture of old western and Indian tunes on an equally diverse mix of Indian reed instruments and battered western brass ones. I once saw a corpse jog by while the band played the old music hall song, 'Hold you hand out, you naughty boy!' I'd love to go like that.

The Anglo-Indian colonies living around the Eliot Road and Ripon Street areas were also a contrasting mixture of the well-off and those who were clearly living hand-to-mouth—though everyone mixed in and there were no caste or class differences. It was sad to see families crammed into a couple of rooms, their possessions placed in every available nook and cranny, eking out an existence, but yet in remarkably good spirits. To meet some of them on the street and at the dances, dressed to impress, you would not know just how badly they

---

[1] Charpoy, literally 'four legs' is a simple string bed with a wooden frame.

were off financially. There was no obvious charity coming their way and most did what they could to try and get by. It was a mystery to me as to how some of them survived. One family I knew, formerly well off because the husband was a doctor, slid down the financial scale when he unexpectedly died. His widow eked out a living by performing illegal back-street abortions with her husband's medical equipment. It is easy to be judgemental, but she had two children to support and life in her basement flat was was hard enough, it flooded in the rains so the family had to sleep on chairs until the water receded a day or two later. She was pretty philosophical about everything and her main consolation was consuming copious amounts of hot black tea.

The hub of Anglo-Indian life was the New Market, a complicated Victorian structure. It was also Calcutta's meeting place—under the New Market clock—whose timekeeping was reasonably reliable and its situation perfect as it was near the flower stalls so you waited in a waft of flower scents that valiantly strove to cover the less agreeable street smells or those coming from the livestock and meat market next door. The market's proper name was the Sir Stuart Hogg Market but nobody ever called it that. The labyrinths and alleyways were crowded with wooden shuttered shops selling everything under the sun. Souvenirs—"Finest quality silver sir? I give you bherry good price!" or, "Look sir, genuine Tibetan painting, if not what about snakeskin handbag for Memsahib? You like a snake Memsahib?" If you looked prosperous and/or foreign, you would be tempted in with offers of tea or cold drinks while the shopkeepers mentally rubbed their hands together in anticipation of fleecing you in the nicest and most charming way possible. There were goods from abroad that looked suspiciously local, silks, underwear, jewellery, perfume, drinks, cakes and clothing. Nahoum's was the bakery of choice for our elaborately decorated Christmas cakes and shocking pink Easter eggs made of a particularly hard icing sugar. We went to the market for curry puffs and small rounds of Bandel cheese made of goat's milk. Then through into the altogether less salubrious animal and bird market where you could buy your chickens and ducks live, and take them home with their feet trussed up, or you could have their necks wrung. You then went round the corner to Free School Street to have your spiced sausages made up by the butcher's there. Stand around in the New Market long enough and you would meet a good proportion of Calcutta's Anglo-Indian population doing their shopping or just spending a leisurely time.

You were never far from reminders of the days of the British Raj. Fort William dominated the river front, the white marble Victoria Memorial dominated the *maidan*[1] and the tall Ochterlony Monument was visible from Chowringhee. There were fine marble statues of former Viceroys and Kings and Queens dotted about—though they were in the process of being removed to a yard behind the race course and replaced by bland statues of post-Independence luminaries almost always with one arm outstretched as though trying to hail one of Calcutta's yellow and black Ambassador taxis. In the atmospheric Park Street cemetery under the crumbling but elaborate tombstones, which indicated that persons of large fortune were interred there, lie the bones of the early British—the sons of Charles Dickens and Captain Cook and Richmond Thackeray, the father of William Makepeace Thackeray, the writer. Perhaps the most poignant is the grave of the Honourable Rose Whitworth Aylmer who died in 1800 aged 20 years. She went to Calcutta to live with her aunt, Lady Russell, the wife of Sir Henry Russell, one of the judges of the Supreme Court after whom Russell Street was named. Before leaving for India she had met the poet Walter Savage Landor who, when he heard of her death, immortalised her in English poetry:

---

[1] A green open space—in Calcutta it runs for miles

> "Ah! What avails the sceptred race?
> Ah! What the form divine?
> What every virtue, every grace?
> Rose Aylmer, all were thine.
> Rose Aylmer, whom these wakeful eyes
> May weep but never see,
> A night of memories and sighs
> I consecrate to thee."

Alas, the Park Street cemetery was crumbling, the marble on the tombs looted to make grinding stones, the poor camping in the grounds among the tombs.

Back in the land of the living, Calcutta went up a gear in the Durga *Puja*[1] season, which was around September, when there would be a succession of noisy processions carrying effigies of the Goddess Kali (also known as Durga) the bringer of death—and life—who is Calcutta's patron goddess. In Hindu mythology, Kali was the wife of Siva, the Destroyer, and when she died the grief-stricken Siva carried her body on his shoulders and began a terrible dance of mourning which threatened to destroy the world as he stamped round it. The god Vishnu, trying to stop this destructive dance, threw a knife at Kali's corpse, cutting it into fifty two pieces which scattered

---

[1] Puja means worship

across the earth. The little toe of her right foot landed by the side of the Hoogly River in Bengal, and a temple was built there. A village grew up around the temple and the people called the place Kalikata. Durga or Kali *puja* culminated in the extravagant painted clay images of Durga/Kali, sometimes several feet tall, being taken from their *pandals*, where they had resided for the past few days, to the river and immersed in the holy waters. The processions were noisy and could sometimes turn violent as rival groups fought for possession of the road to the river. The artistry of the image makers is now being recognised worldwide. A couple of summers ago in London they brought over some image-makers who constructed an image of the Goddess Kali, which was then immersed in the Thames.

The political situation in Calcutta had been getting increasingly volatile. The Communists were in power and the general level of violence was increasing. An extreme left-wing group, the Naxalites, named after a place called Naxalbari where they had originated, began kidnapping and killing rich land-owners in the countryside. The Statesman was a regular target for demonstrators because of the paper's strong opposition to Mrs Gandhi, the Prime Minister, who we criticised for becoming increasingly dictatorial, or for its criticism of Calcutta's communist administration. We were being attacked at least once a week by mobs throwing stones and bottles and home-made bombs and trying to force their way into the building. My office overlooked the street outside and had wire mesh over the windows to protect the glass from damage. The door to the building was a revolving one made of heavy Burma teak and the office messengers, the 'peons', would barricade the door, sometimes jamming the demonstrators in it.

A favourite weapon on the streets of Calcutta was the soda water bottle—these were shaken and then thrown, to explode with a bang, scattering glass all around. In India, where the wearing of shoes was not the norm, this had a profound effect. The more organised thugs filled electric light bulbs with acid and flung them around. When a demonstration got particularly violent, the police would arrive and usually make a '*lathi* charge' on the crowd—*lathis* are iron-tipped bamboo staves. On rare occasions they would open fire, first shooting a warning above the heads of the mob. If the mob did not heed the warning the police would fire into them, panicking them into flight and leaving the untidy bodies of the killed and wounded behind. It would merit a few paragraphs in the next day's news—but there was never a call for an investigation into the Police action. After a while we became a bit blasé about the violence outside our windows and just went about our normal business.

There were also periodic riots between Hindus and Muslims which resulted in mass killings. Anyone who has lived through them can never forget the roars of the crowds as they stormed a Muslim or Hindu area, followed by the screams of the people being killed. The next day, on the way to work, we would pass the bodies lying in the streets. During these periods of sectarian violence Gurkha troops were brought in—they were religiously neutral—and a night curfew was imposed. I was occasionally required to report for work at night in the press room—which was short-staffed as many of the Hindu and Muslim staff remained home with their families. Journeys to and from work were in the newspaper's vans, we were locked into the windowless rear compartment, and we could hear the crowds outside chanting and shouting and sometimes there would be the heavy thud of a stone or brickbat against the van's sides. It was a very scary experience. We often debated what we would do if the van was stopped. The usual drill to identify whether a person was Hindu or Muslim was to get them to drop their trousers—Muslims were circumcised. As Anglo-Indians we were not sure where we stood and whether old anti-Raj feelings would take hold and a mob, of whatever religious persuasion, would turn on us anyway.

As you can see, life at The Statesman was never dull. I was an 'Executive' in the Advertising Department—

which was the money-spinning part of the newspaper. Advertising makes far more money than the cover price of the paper, which is why so many newspapers in the West are given away free. I spent most of my time editing classified advertisements and checking that they did not violate the law. We had to be careful, for example, not to allow pictures of famous people, or claims that they endorsed the product. Nor could advertisers offer prizes or run competitions without getting permission from the authorities. There were rogue members of the public who tried to misuse our columns. One Irish lady, eccentric by all accounts, would pay for personal classified adverts to celebrate the birth of the Irish Republic or the Easter Uprising—at the end of which she would include a line in Gaelic. Once she included a line that was definitely not Gaelic, "Disis apisp otana tinwuntu" (say it running the words together—the spelling may not be correct but the meaning is clear). We caught it just in time, so to speak, and never allowed her anything but English in future. She was totally unrepentant.

It was an old-fashioned organisation. In those days there were no computers and the nearest we got to anything mechanical in my office was the typewriter and telephone (which was controlled by an Operator). I would tinkle a bell on my desk to get the peons to come and clear my 'out tray' or to run errands. The newspaper was produced on banks of Linotype machines, which were mechanical typesetters that produced 'slugs' of type in cast metal. These were assembled in pages on a 'stone', a sturdy steel table, and a papier mache 'flong' was pressed on to the page to make a reverse impression of it. This was then curved and filled with molten metal to make a semi-circular printing block to go on the presses. The print room, presided over by Mr Moore, was an incredibly exciting place filled with energy and urgency, the clatter of machinery and the smell of hot type. Nowadays newspapers are done quietly by computer.

I was trained when I first came, by two Anglo-Indians, Bev Pearson and then Jean Ross. They were both delightful people but, unfortunately, left shortly after I joined to emigrate. In came Chandran Nair, a young chap from South India who was my age; we rapidly became the best of friends. The Deputy Ad Manager was a tall Anglo-Indian called Ron, who was a keen golfer and, in what passed for the winter in Calcutta, got up early to practice for the annual Statesman employees' golf tournament. Ron would talk endlessly about his practice sessions and ostentatiously leave two golf balls on his desk—which led to ribald comments such as, "Ah Ron, I see you've shot another golf", or we would mimic golf swings when passing his desk shielding our eyes with a hand to watch the flight of an imaginary ball only—shock, horror—to look down and indicate that we had missed it! As Ron took his golf seriously, he was not amused. One year, a player dropped out of the tournament and a passing sports reporter was persuaded to fill his place. This chap had never played golf before but gave it a go. He ended up with a better score than Ron, which was a source of great amusement for weeks. Ron duly emigrated to Australia—I don't think it was because of the golf score. Ron briefly became the Acting Advertising Manager after our boss, Alec Marsh, a quiet and somewhat reserved Englishman, also took his leave and retired to the UK.

The Ad Manager's vacancy was filled by 'Our man in Bombay', Chandran Tharoor, who was energetic, well-connected and determined to modernise the Ad Department and go after as much advertising revenue as possible. His son, Shashi, who used to come into the paper as a small child to visit his father, stood last year for the General Secretaryship of the United Nations. Among his initiatives, Tharoor decided to introduce Matrimonial advertisements—The Statesman had resisted carrying these on grounds of taste, even though they were a common feature of other Indian newspapers. The Board of Directors took a lot of convincing. There was a feeling that The Statesman was above such a thing. We persuaded the Board that the newspaper's reputation for fairness and honesty was a distinct advantage here, as we would be thoroughly scrutinising the adverts to ensure that they were genuine. To convince the Board, Tharoor asked me to draft a letter that could go out to potential advertisers setting out the advantages of using The Statesman—and used these arguments to get his proposal through. We cleverly sent this letter in reply to the box numbers of the adverts placed in other papers—and generated a huge volume of business as a result.

I was also given a free hand to design bigger advertising campaigns for clients. I had begun persuading small manufacturers to buy more advertising space, suggesting ideas to them for ad campaigns, which I would sketch out for them. This led to my designing the adverts and writing the copy, and the Art Department would do the finished artwork. This part of our work expanded and became more successful and we began operating as a small advertising agency. Advertising in India has to be capable of translation into the other Indian languages besides English, so it is best to avoid alliteration and puns. There was an elaborate campaign for Amul butter, not done by me, I add, whose slogan was: 'Better buy Amul because you can't buy better butter.' Got lost in translation, I think. One of my early efforts was for a company that re-treaded tyres. I used the slogan: 'We tread carefully,' illustrated by footprints showing tyre treads—in India cheap slippers were made from the rubber of tyres. No, it wasn't a world beater!

Around this time the Beatles were very successful and there was growing interest in pop music and teenage culture. Evan Charlton, The Statesman's Editor, decided to set up a weekly magazine aimed at teenagers. After tossing around various suggestions for names, the powers that be decided on the seriously un-cool 'Junior Statesman'. This opened up a new avenue for me as I was heavily involved in my own pop group and had a good knowledge of the British and American pop scenes. The newspaper recruited a small team of young people to run the magazine under the editorship of Desmond Doig—a lovely, approachable, man who was an immensely talented writer and artist. I began writing articles and short stories for the new magazine and designing adverts to promote it.

Doig persuaded the newspaper to buy an old Model-T Ford car, which was painted in psychedelic colours—mostly a vile orange—and then offered as a prize to the readers. This generated enormous publicity for the magazine and subsequently led to the newspaper sponsoring an annual vintage car rally.

Doig encouraged me to write more creatively. So much so that in fact the most creative piece I wrote was a description of a concert that I decided not to attend as it clashed with a party I was going to. A friend who used the free tickets I was given, told me about the concert and I wrote my piece based partly on his information. Doig loved it and I still have his note of appreciation. If only he knew! The writing in the Junior Statesman was of exceptional quality. Doig's own efforts were boosted by those of two of his principal writers—Dubby Bhagat (whose father was General Bhagat VC) and Jug Suraya, who is now well known as a columnist for The Times of India.

It was a fun place to work in and my colleagues in The Statesman were a lively mix, we were all thoroughly devoted to the company and were immensely proud of our newspaper and our magazine. We also met socially outside work. I loved working there.

Early in 1967, the newspaper was hit by a *'gherao'*—a Bengali word for when the employees' lock in' the senior staff as a form of industrial dispute—a tactic which had suddenly become fashionable. We executive staff lived a privileged life. A car picked me up from home each morning and dropped me back at night. I had a key to the Executive Lavatory (yes, really) and ate lunch in the Executives' Dining Room on starched linen, while being waited on by uniformed waiters. There was a passion for *gheraos* at the time and almost every company of note had had one, its workers no doubt encouraged by the existence of the communist government in Bengal. So, expressing concerns about poor pay, but no doubt envious of the perks enjoyed by the management, our employees locked us in one afternoon. The police had to come and free us later that night—our staff did not attack us but simply barricaded the exits and the Directors in their offices. The newspaper's management shut the paper down and prepared to sit out the dispute until the staff gave in. In the weeks that followed we would meet, together with the other executives, in one or other of the Director's houses each day and do as much work as we could, which was not very much as the newspaper was not being published in Calcutta, though we continued to feed the Delhi edition. At this time I got the results of the Advertising Training Course that the newspaper had sponsored me on—I had won the Gold Medal.

After a month the dispute ended as the poor staff were by now penniless and were forced to concede and return to work. In the morning, as I got ready to go back for the first time, there was a knock on my door and I opened it to find one of my Bengali clerks. He advised me not to go in with the rest of the executives but to go in about 30 minutes later as trouble was anticipated. Intrigued, I went in early and watched from a distance. As the executives arrived, they were set on by the frustrated employees and the most unpopular were beaten, the rest roughly shoved and pushed. Only three of us, all Anglo-Indians, were given advance warning because, I presume, we were liked by our staff.

Our staff were, naturally, mainly Bengalis, the archetypal 'Bengali Babus', many of them very well educated and extremely cultured. These were men who read Rabindranath Tagore and both Indian and English classical literature for pleasure and who were steeped in Bengali art and music. They adored the films of Satyajit Ray and introduced me to them. What they must have made of usurpers like me, wet behind the ears, who were placed in positions over them I do not know—they were far too nice and polite to say. I found them very helpful and engaging—sometimes startling as there was an undercurrent of both caste and colour prejudice that was part of their makeup. For example, we had two junior clerks with the same surname, let's say, Biswas. They were commonly known as Biswas and *Kala* Biswas (black Biswas). The senior clerks had a big influence in recruiting their staff and this is where caste was often a deciding factor, not to mention ensuring that relatives got first pick.

The two senior clerks introduced me to the works of Tagore, a Bengali from a very distinguished family who had won the Nobel Prize for literature in 1913 for his work, Gitanjali (Song Offerings). He is famous for his songs, art, stories plays and poems. With his cheque from the Nobel Prize he founded an experimental school at Shantinikethan, which still exists. He was also influential in the Independence movement, advocating cooperation between the East and West while Gandhi was advocating non-cooperation. I like him best for his lyrical poetry which brings alive the simplicity of rural India with all its pain and sweetness. Some of his poetry is quoted in this book. Whenever I read his work I feel nostalgic for the India I knew.

Paddy got her degree in the summer of 1968 (BA Honours in English). That December we married in Loreto College Church, Middleton Row. As a non-Catholic I had to sign a form promising to bring up any children as Catholics—which I have singularly failed to keep. My best friend, Chandran Nair[1], a Hindu from Kerala, who had never been inside a church in his life, was my best man—I think he was more nervous than I was. The bride wore a golden (with real gold) sari and we held the reception at her father's house—he had become the manager of the Government Printing Press in Calcutta and had a large colonial flat with a wide verandah all round it, situated just behind the High Court. Paddy and I paid for everything—I had to sell my trea-

---

[1] His full name is Kannambra Balachandran Nair, which is quite difficult to say if you are not familiar with Tamil or Malayalam. We called him K B or Chandran.

sured, noisy motor-cycle to afford it. Paddy's decision to wear a sari rather than a traditional bridal dress reflected our love of and commitment to India—we felt that our future lay there and were comfortable and secure in our jobs and our friendships. We were very much an equal part of a multi-cultural society—our friends and acquaintances were Hindus, Muslims, Sikhs, Indian Christians, Anglo-Indians, Nepalese and Parsees.

We moved into our own flat on the huge Karnani Estate on Lower Circular Road near Park Circus. This was leased to me by the newspaper. I was in their good books as I had done a lot of work in helping them with the teenage magazine—and had secured a number of good advertising contracts by designing well received ad campaigns for clients. The Gold Medal and support through the gherao had also helped. The flat was basically one very large room which we divided with a curtain to separate the sitting room from the sleeping area. We had a balcony, which we enclosed to create a dressing room and two small cubicles either side of the front door which doubled as kitchen area and storage. There was a bathroom, but the water only ran for a couple of hours each day so we left the tap on to fill a large oil drum which doubled as our water storage. We hired all our furniture from Mitra Sales Bureau on Wellesley Street—hiring your furniture for a small monthly payment was common in Calcutta, and very economical. So began our life together.

We were able to entertain our friends at home for the first time and did so several times a week—when we were not out on the town at Trincas or the cinema, or paying return visits to our friends. We had an elderly woman, somewhat destitute, who used to sleep in the corridor outside our flat. She appeared to do a little work for a couple of the other tenants and in return was given food. We did not much like the idea of having someone virtually living in the corridor, but there was nowhere for the poor woman to go. It did not last long. In the early hours I was woken by a strange sound and realised that it was the death rattle of the poor woman. We rushed outside but it was too late. The tenants donated money for her cremation. Her life was tragic, her death was tragic—it was Calcutta.

Paddy found she was pregnant a few months after we had married, so we acquired an ayah, Kathleen, who turned out to be a real gem. She was the daughter of the ayah who had looked after Paddy's brother's children. Kathleen insisted on cooking our meals as well as looking after our son, Maric, who arrived the following September—even though this was not in her job description. Her husband, Lawrence, came in at weekends to do odd jobs for us—as a couple they were very genuine and trustworthy. They paid us a great compliment when we were about to leave India by inviting us to lunch at their *bustee* (slum dwelling). We went along, with some trepidation, but were delighted at the reception we got and were able to meet Kathleen's other children. We were truly sad to leave Lawrence and her behind.

11

The Calcutta Scene

Calcutta, for all its poverty, crowds and decay, was also one of the most interesting and entertaining cities in which to live. It had the largest Anglo-Indian population of any city in India, mostly clustered around a few areas: Eliot Road, Ripon Street, Wellesley Street and its lanes, Free School Street, Park Circus, Dhurumtollah, Bow Bazaar and across the river in Howrah in the railway colony. The richer Anglo-Indians, and some were very rich, lived in the posher suburbs such as Ballygunge. Paddy's family had owned or rented property for decades in Eliot Road—across from the Lawrence Funeral Parlour.

The Anglo-Indian community was very active socially. There were regular dances, known as 'shows', at the Rangers Club and the Grail Club almost every Saturday, there were house parties to go to, people visited the restaurants and night clubs on fashionable Park Street and it was common to visit one's friends at home without giving them advance notice—there weren't many telephones around, so ringing up was not always an option. After church on Sundays, families visited one another and usually ended up having a traditional lunch of chicken curry and pilau or ball curry[1] and yellow rice. The main alcohol was rum (Gurkha rum was the best and strongest), gin or Solan No. 1 Whisky, all produced in India, and of course Bangalore beer. Very occasionally, we younger people would, for a laugh, drink cheap country hooch, arak, distilled from toddy palms. As this was illegal, it was sometimes smuggled in via the inner tubes of bicycle or car tyres, which gave it a horrible rubbery taste and smell. The only way it could be made remotely palatable was to dilute it with Coca-Cola. We avoided the cruder forms of country liquor or stuff made with methylated spirits or even shoe polish—did the drinkers sniff it appreciatively and comment on the bouquet of the Kiwi '68 Dark Tan, I wonder? There were too

---

[1] known in our family as 'spinster's delight', a friend told me it was known in his as 'bad word' curry.

many reports of drinkers of these strange beverages going blind.

The Anglo-Indian has a reputation for living for the day and a common saying was that if you had two Anglo-Indians and a glass of lime juice you had a party. And boy, did we have some good parties! I've been to ones in people's houses where they had a live band—I remember Pop Booth's band, and can still hear his sax—as well as the radiogram blasting out with a mixture of the latest records, Sinatra standards, and the sentimental Jim Reeves and Tony Brent songs. Our rock group was often invited to play live at the bigger 'house parties' and the European clubs (to which we would ordinarily never have been admitted). The 'house parties' were, so far as I could see, mainly open house with scores of people turning up having heard through the grapevine. Nobody was turned away—provided they brought a bottle of booze with them. Our band's services were paid for in free booze and food. The din from these parties was horrendous but nobody seemed to complain.

We were also invited to the Golden Slipper nightclub, near the Elite cinema, where, for a time, they held late night private discotheques once a week ('discotheque' was a new word then) which went on till dawn and had the most up to date pop hits from the UK and USA to dance to. Whoever organised these sessions was very choosy about who was invited and there was usually a good party crowd drawn from Calcutta's nightclub performers and their friends. Sadly, the Golden Slipper is no more and is now the Hotel Raunak.

The foreign sailors used to frequent Isiah's Bar on Free School Street. In all my time in Calcutta I never went there—the general view was that it was a place frequented by prostitutes and there were certainly a lot of dubious looking people going in and out of the entrance door. It was not the sort of place to which you would dream of taking a date, or even admit to having been in.

Visits to the cinema were regular, at least once a week for the 6 o'clock or 9 o'clock show—the Lighthouse, New Empire, Elite or Metro mostly—followed by a visit to Nizam's for a *kathi kebab*—barbecued meat, fresh onions and chillies rolled in a *paratha*—or a *kiri kebab*, which was made from the meat of cows' udders. Ask any Calcutta Anglo-Indian about them, it will always bring back fond memories. There are many *kathi* shops in Calcutta but Nizam's was by far the best. It seemed to stay open through the night—I can remember leaving house parties in the early hours with friends and taking a taxi to Nizam's because we felt like having a *kathi* and they did not disappoint. Another classic culinary treat, peculiar to Bengal, was *puchkas*, also known as *pani purees*, small deep fried bubbles of dough which were pierced by the street vendor's (usually grimy) thumb and filled with a potato, spice and lentil mixture, all of which was hand-dipped into spicy tamarind water and deposited into a conical cup made of a leaf, which you held. It was also possible to buy *kulfis*, which were delicious, very creamy cardamom flavoured ice creams, usually made in metal cones which the vendor would rub furiously in his hands to thaw slightly to release the frozen contents. The more adventurous could have a '*bhang kulfi*', a dusting of bhang (cannabis) was applied on top just as we in the west would apply nuts and sprinkles. Cannabis and opium were sold legally through state run shops and many an ayah would insert a small dab of cannabis or opium between the gum and lower lip of her infant charge to keep it placid. Memsahib was usually none the wiser.

Park Street was the nerve centre of Calcutta's western-style entertainment. It had a good choice of restaurants—Trincas, Magnolias, the Blue Fox, Mogambos (just off Park Street, with its red rexine sofas), Kwality's, Moulin Rouge (where there was a troupe of can-can dancers I recall)—and later on the Park Hotel. Almost every place had a band that played jazz standards and Broadway hits and had a resident 'crooner', usually female who came with her own devoted collection of fans. The most famous were Pat Tarley, Pam Crain, Brenda Lilley, Yvonne

Arden, Eve, Ripsy, Shirley Churcher and 'Delicious Delovely Delilah' who also ran the Moulin Rouge! Backing them were some very good bands—the most memorable for me were Cecil Dorsey's, Sonny Lobo's and Joe Pereira's orchestras. I also remember Tony Menezes and Dominic D'Costa. There were also cabaret artistes: Vivian Hansen, Reuben Rebeiro, Jack Pianowski (The Klassic Komic of the Krazy Keys), Mike Danton (who sang and did impersonations), Markus the Magician. The Blue Fox has recently become a McDonald's burger restaurant, serving the McAloo Tikki! Shoot me if it ever starts serving the McAloo Chop.

A number of Anglo-Indian girls performed a tame sort of strip-tease, usually going down to skimpy bikinis. The most popular was Luscious Lola, who liked a drink and apparently could sometimes be so tanked up at show time and so enthusiastic that it was always a guessing game as to whether she would remember to stop stripping when she reached her last skimpy bikini—as a full striptease was forbidden. Being in a rock band, we got to see rather more of these strip-tease cabaret performers in the dressing rooms! They too had their devoted following of fans, mostly the young British managers who worked for the jute mills that lined the Hoogly river. They would be invited to their homes after the night's cabaret had ended, usually after midnight, and would drag us along as protection! It was nice to see how the other half lived with their extravagant flats and Ferrograph tape recorders—the latest thing—with electrostatic speakers. We were more interested in hearing the latest hits from the UK so that we could copy them and sing them in public before anybody else did. Alas, the young managers found themselves out of luck with the girls.

As a musician, I played most of the Park Street venues with the Wild Ones or with other bands that needed a bass player. For a while we were the resident group at the jam sessions in the Moulin Rouge, where the owner, Delilah, allowed us to do whatever we wanted—including not batting an eyelid when one of us jumped up and stood on the piano to sing. The more informal the jam sessions became, the bigger the crowds. The Sunday afternoon 'jam sessions' were popular as the bands played a mixture of jazz standards and rock 'n' roll and people loved to dance. The restaurants were usually packed and the food of choice was the triple-decker club sandwich with fried cashew nuts on the side. The clientele were well heeled Indians living off Daddy's money, expat English and, of course, Anglo-Indians. Night club and restaurant hopping was a popular pastime, often ending late at night at Kwality's for an ice cream or a *'pan'*—areca nut, quick lime and other stuff wrapped in a betel leaf—considered a digestive, or Nizam's for a *kathi*.

I recently read an article in a Calcutta paper which looked back at the Swinging Sixties in Calcutta. It sadly noted of the bandsmen, singers and cabaret artistes of the day who had remained in Cal, "While some turned to alcohol or drugs, many died of starvation." Can you believe that? If it's true it is awful. The more fortunate ones moved on to Bombay or into the Bollywood film scene as musicians. A guy called Noel Martin, whom I knew when he sang with Mike Booth's Tornadoes, is still playing in Trincas with his band, Sweet Agitation. He has been there for 21 years; all the members of his band are a lot younger than he is. He is pessimistic about his future, "I have a large family and no savings. The situation is the same for many guys like me." With no savings or pensions and investments solely in musical instruments, old age looks bleak.

A more sedate scene was that of the mixed groups of upmarket Indians and Anglo-Indians who were members of the Calcutta Light Opera Group and The Amateurs drama group. They too held frequent house parties and we usually subscribed towards the food and drink. There was an interesting mix of people at these parties from young people like myself in or just out of college, to senior industrialists and officers from the armed services or police. Molly Kaye—the writer M M Kaye of The Far Pavilions—was a regular for a while.

Most of the people were a lot older than me but all of us got on well together—though I do remember an occasion when a tough as nails British Gurkha officer held a young chap upside down out of an upstairs window because he thought he had been flirting with his wife! The evenings were rounded off with an impromptu sing-song of pieces from recent shows.

I developed a taste for Indian classical music through regular visits with my friend, Chandran, to the home of one of The Statesman's sub-editors, Surinder Varma, who was also Deputy Editor of the Junior Statesman and was responsible for ensuring the good quality of its writing. Surinder was a small, dapper man with glasses, very well educated and with a keen sense of humour. He had spent some time in England working as a journalist. He was a member of the Cochin royal family but was completely free of airs and graces and was very well liked for his professional approach and light touch. I really enjoyed his company. He loved having us to dinner at his home where his delightful wife, Padmini, would spoil us and cook us wonderful south Indian food; and we would end the evening drinking South Indian coffee and listening to a wide variety of Indian classical music, whose nuances Surinder would explain to us. I didn't know, for example, that ragas played in the morning could only draw on a particular set of musical notes. Or that the *ghatham*, a round earthenware pot, used like a drum, relied on the player having a big enough belly to push up against the mouth of the instrument whose tone he varied by moving his belly in and out.

One weekend the Varma family, Chandran and I went to the seaside resort of Digha. We travelled down on the Saturday afternoon after work in the Varma's car and stayed overnight. On our way back the next evening the car blew a radiator hose and we had to pull in to a *dak* bungalow—a rest house from colonial days with its heavy Victorian furniture, gloomy lighting and old fashioned *punkahs* hanging from the cobwebbed ceilings, but with nobody around to pull them to create a stir of air. We needed to get a new hose for the car so Chandran and I elected to go back to Calcutta by bus and train. We would get the part and one of us would return with it—the other would stay on at work as both of us couldn't be absent at the same time. The journey back was a nightmare and we sat on the floor in a crowded third class railway compartment—it was the best we could do as we had taken little money with us. I attracted some strange looks as I was wearing Indian clothes, a kurtha pyjama and slippers, but was not obviously Indian and the age of the European hippie had yet to dawn. Chandran got back with the hose the next day and the situation was saved.

I also spent a lot of my time socialising with old school

and college friends. We went round on our motor-bikes and scooters, girl friends on the pillions. Those without transport took taxis and these strange convoys would wend our way round the city, perhaps to the river front for fresh air and *puchkas*, or to the *maidan* just to sit out or sometimes for a picnic. Evenings were usually spent in each other's houses, or in dining at one of the restaurants and nightclubs.

Horse racing was very popular, and there were two racetracks. The main Calcutta race course was a very professional affair run under Jockey Club rules. It attracted numerous foreign riders, some quite famous, escaping the European winter. I used to see them in Firpo's dancing with their invariably tall and statuesque wives. (A British comedian recently asked, "Jockeys, experienced and talented equestrian sportsmen, or little buggers hanging on for dear life?") A number of Anglo-Indian lads joined the jockey training school set up by the Calcutta racecourse and had reasonably successful careers. The centre of the racecourse was used as a polo field and I would sometimes wander along to see the teams do their stuff. It was not a popular sport and didn't really catch on despite its long history in India.

Then there was the Tollygunge Racecourse, which encircled the snooty Tollygunge Golf Club. This was a strictly amateur affair and a boy from my class in school,

Alan Tyabji, who came from a wealthy racehorse-owning family was one of the very successful riders there. Tollygunge was a strange experience. The start of each race could be glimpsed through the trees behind the golf clubhouse. Then the riders disappeared behind the clubhouse, which was when, it was alleged, that a bit of naughtiness took place and horses were 'pulled' to ensure that the result was rigged. The finish line lacked any form of equipment other than a tightly strung wire from floor to ceiling in the judges' box to enable them to determine which horse's nose had crossed the line first. I have actually seen a jockey standing up in the finish straight and pulling hard on the reigns to slow the favourite down as the insider money was on another horse. Of course this led to periodic riots among the disgruntled punters when the furniture would be flung about and the tote buildings stormed.

The head man in charge of the betting operation at Tollygunge was 'Uncle Harold' Chew, who was married to my wife's aunt. Uncle Harold was, in real life, an eminent tea taster for Lyons, very well respected. He was a small Chinese with very forthright opinions. Despite the wonderful cooking of his wife, Ercy, he never put on weight—mostly because of his nervous restless energy. He must have had a very tough job keeping the angry Tollygunge punters in check.

Christmas in Calcutta was a big affair for both Anglo-Indians and Indians. It kicked off in early December and carried on until early January—by which time a lot of money had been spent, alcohol drunk, shows and parties attended and families were reduced to living on 'dhall and rice' until they could recover their finances. Park Street and the New Market were lavishly decorated and the number of parties and 'shows' reached a crescendo. Groups of us went carol singing, but only visiting the houses of people we knew, being invited in for sherry or homemade alcoholic drinks and very alcoholic Christmas cake made to the family's secret recipe, until we staggered home quite smashed in the early hours. There was no question of people pretending to be out when carol singers called—they loved any excuse for an impromptu party.

Everyone aspired to have new clothes for Christmas and the New Market was abuzz with Christmas shoppers for clothing, food, toys and gifts. People also clamoured for the hot tickets to the Rangers or Grail clubs' lavish Christmas and New Year's Eve dances—they were 'the event' to be seen at as a good time was guaranteed. The poor *durzis* (tailors) worked overtime as all the dresses were individually tailor made, and to the latest fashions. The *durzis* were amazing, often producing dresses based on nothing more than an illustration in a magazine. The hairdressers were busy on the day—bouffant styles were in fashion and the smell of spray lacquer in the women's hair was overpowering. Running your fingers through your date's hair was simply not possible.

The Rangers Club dances were special affairs. Tickets sold out well in advance and everyone turned up dressed in their smartest. There was a fashion among young men for a few years in the 60s to wear cream coloured shirts and black drain-pipe trousers with Beatle boots made by the Chinese shoemakers of Bentinck Street, so we all did it and it became an unofficial evening dress. Dancing was to live bands, and my band was sometimes on the bill. On one occasion Frank Anthony was the guest of honour at a dance at which I was playing and asked to meet me. I refused point blank, given that he had sacked my father—silly, in retrospect. At around midnight everyone attending the dance would have a buffet dinner of *kathi* kebabs and samosas, or curry and *pulao* or yellow rice, before resuming dancing till dawn. Almost everyone knew everyone. It was practically traditional for a fight to break out, usually over some girl. Things would get heated for a few minutes and then would cool down. The police were never called nor the protagonists ejected.

I once did a gig with the Fathoms at the Railway Institute in Asansol, a big railway town, where Paddy was in school in the Loreto Convent—though I didn't know her then. It began with a dreadful embarrassment. The Institute had sent the band the money for First Class rail tickets (they had originally promised third class ones, but we demanded better), we pocketed the difference and got ourselves Third Class tickets. When the train drew up at Asansol station, we were shocked to find a good proportion of the local Anglo-Indian population had turned out to meet us—only to find us emerging sheepishly from Third Class. We need not have worried, the First Class tickets were freebies anyway as it was a railway Institute—and there was intense competition among the crowd to have a member of the group use their home to shower in and get ready for the dance. I ended up in the home of one of the families, who had no door on their bathroom, only a curtain. The daughter of the family was keen to impress as she had a good singing voice and later went on to do some cabaret singing in Calcutta—however, she lacked the glamorous appearance that the nightclubs wanted from their female singers. She had a face made for radio, as the expression goes.

The dance we were playing at was like stepping back in time for me because, in addition to the jive and the twist, the railway crowd loved old time dancing and expertly performed dances like The Lancers and The Gay Gordons which belonged to another era—yet everyone knew the steps. Of course there was the traditional fight, settled outside the hall, with the bloodied combatants coming back to the dance as if nothing had happened in time for the midnight samosas. A good time was definitely had by all.

12

Blighty Bound

As the political situation and violence worsened in Calcutta under the communist government, and the country drifted into a sort of dictatorship under Prime Minister Indira Gandhi, it was becoming more and more obvious that the Anglo-Indians no longer fitted in. Anglo-Indian men were finding it increasingly difficult to get decent jobs and families were often sustained by the wives, mothers and sisters working as secretaries or telephonists—jobs in which they excelled, but which did not pay handsomely.

The Government began trying to limit the number of European expats employed in The Statesman—we had some very influential expat journalists who were critical of the Government and opposed Indira Gandhi's dictatorial style of leadership and began putting pressure on the paper to reduce their numbers. The exodus to the UK, Canada and Australia gathered pace, and in the late 1960s, people who had intended to remain in India, like Paddy and myself, changed their minds and began applying to emigrate. To get to the UK you had to have at least a grandparent who was British born—which posed no problem for us, and I was a registered British citizen. Those who might have difficulty in meeting the conditions for the UK opted for Canada or Australia, using the influence of their church as the priests had connections abroad who were willing to act as sponsors.

Almost every week we heard of families who had left or were in the process of leaving. There was an efficient grapevine operating and news of departures quickly got around. You would notice absences at the dances, and I sometimes got first hand information that people were leaving when they called in at The Statesman to place adverts to sell their possessions or to announce their departure. There was a real sense that the community was shrinking fast. This intensified the pressure on those left behind to emigrate also as they could see the world rapidly changing round them.

Some families simply didn't have the money for the fares. They sold everything and saved and borrowed—

anything to afford to emigrate. One or two were more ingenious. We heard tales of desperate people who worked a scam on the Kabuli (Afghan) moneylenders. The Kabulis were a staple source of borrowing (at extortionate rates) for the poorer families. It was a common sight to see hordes of Kabulis in their distinctive dress and turbans congregating together on the Calcutta *maidan* each Sunday to socialise and to compare notes on who was a bad debtor and who was not.

The way the scam was operated was as follows: the family would borrow a small sum of money, and pay it back well on time and with full interest. They would do this a number of times over a few months, building a relationship with the Kabuli and spinning tales of waiting to move into a plum job etc. They might do this to several Kabulis, moving money borrowed from one to pay off another. They would then suddenly up the amount of money borrowed from each. The Kabulis would be told to turn up on a particular day (usually earlier than the normal repayment period). By then, of course, the family, having got its money together would have left India. It didn't take long for the Kabulis to get wise to this. One or two families cut it fine and were pursued to the airport.

Paddy and I decided to leave India when we knew back in February 1969 that she was pregnant. In some ways it was a crazy decision. We would have had no trouble furthering our careers in India, she was working for Union Carbide (makers of Eveready batteries) and The Statesman had indicated a promising career for me. However, we felt that our child's future would not be so secure the way things were going. I held a British passport by virtue of my grandfather being born in the UK, and my parents were in England—so emigration to the UK was the obvious choice for us. Our son, Maric[1], was born in September 1969 and we began our plans to leave by the summer of the next year. Emigration was also being considered by Paddy's family. Her cousins had already left for Canada, courtesy of the church's sponsorship, and her aunts intended to follow. Her sister, Babs, was thinking about following her in-laws to Australia. And even Carl, who was doing very well with his company, by now had three children and was beginning to think that his and their future did not lie in India.

I had a difficult conversation at work with The Statesman's Managing Director when I tendered my resignation. He wanted to know why I was leaving and was deeply hurt as the newspaper had great plans for me and my career. I couldn't really say, "Sorry, but I don't really fit in with this country anymore," because clearly I did fit in

---

[1] a combination of Marjorie and Eric, my parents' names.

and could have made a big success of my life in India. Nor could I say, "I'm going because my child doesn't have a future in India." It was something he would not have understood—that it was time for people like us to move on. Instead, I said I was leaving for health reasons as I needed to have my eye seen to because of the damage to my retina. He was very kind and gave me a great reference.

The Indian Government does not particularly want you to stay but also does not make it easy for you to leave. They only allowed departing Anglo-Indians to take out £3 in foreign currency for each family member, so we had no option but to give our possessions away and leave our money behind as the Rupee was worthless abroad. Before you are cleared to go, the Government requires a statement from the tax inspector that says you do not owe them any outstanding tax—the dreaded tax clearance certificate. This is easier said than done. Despite my and Paddy's companies providing a full account of our salaries and tax payments over the years, I had to hire a tax lawyer and provide him with 'bribe money' to grease the palms of the bureaucracy. He said that he needed first to bribe the clerks to find my tax file. Disbelieving, I went with him to the Government file registry, near Writer's Building, which turned out to be a large room, the size of a ballroom, crammed to the ceiling with files, apparently in no particular order. Without any cash incentive it could have taken years for my file to have been found—so they said.

It was a joke that a Babu who worked for the 'Vest Bengal Gawrment' will arrive at 10 o'clock, wipe his perspiring forehead till 11, have a tea break at 12, throw around a few files at 12.30, break for lunch at 1, smoke an unfiltered cigarette at 2, break for tea at 3, sleep sitting down at 4 and go home at 4.30. Hard life!

Then my lawyer had to bribe tax officials to ensure that the necessary checks and calculations were done speedily. We were given the run around, being required to attend a series of interviews with the tax inspector, until the morning we were due to leave Calcutta and I missed my farewell party at The Statesman—this I very much regretted as I wanted to say goodbye to my many friends there. At the eleventh hour, the tax inspector claimed that he needed a statement from Paddy's employers—I rushed to her office and persuaded a secretary we knew to write me the necessary statement on headed notepaper, I duly signed it myself, pretending to be one of the company's officials, and we got the necessary clearance.

The tax people had refined this subtle form of torture and I am sure many of you reading this book who emigrated from India will have your own horror stories of how difficult life was made for you before you got your final clearance. Common to all the stories I heard was that of being kept waiting until the last minute—some unlucky ones had to delay their departure—and I heard stories of tax officials taking a shine to someone's shirt, or pen or lighter, which subsequently had to be presented to the official in order to keep things moving. I think I was lucky because I dropped broad hints that my father in law was a big-wig in the Government—which he was—and that if I chose to I could write about my experiences in The Statesman—probably less accurate.

As we could not take many possessions with us since we were leaving by air, we crated up some of them, mainly linen, and sent them by sea. The rest we simply gave away to our friends as it was pointless to sell them as we could not take the money out of the country. We left money in bank accounts, and there are probably thousands of such accounts still open in India.

We went to Delhi to spend a week with Paddy's parents before flying to the UK. I went to look at the Frank Anthony Public School, which you may recall was still being built when we had left it in 1961. I could hardly recognise the place as the open spaces and fields where we had once roamed free were now covered in dense housing. The sadhu was still there, however, they hadn't yet demolished his Mughal tomb.

We left India with very mixed feelings. We were leaving behind family and close friends. We loved the country, it was the country of our birth and it was all we had ever known, but we realised that we were increasingly out of place there. Nehru's Independence speech had spelt it out clearly, our age in India had ended. The country we loved with its multitude of castes and religions viewed us as an unwanted reminder of its colonial past. We couldn't and wouldn't submerge our history and character to become more Indian, so there was only one choice. Our sadness was tempered by the excitement of a new beginning, moving from the third world to the first, to the promise of a better future. Not quite returning 'home' because we regarded India as our home, but a return to a people from whom we drew our origins and culture.

Our last memento of India was a brass Buddha head which we bought at Delhi Airport to use up our Indian money. It stands in our sitting room—he's gazed benignly over us ever since.

> *Then finish the last song and let us leave,*
> *Forget this night when the night is no more,*
> *Whom do I try to clasp in my arms? Dreams can never be made captive.*
> *My eager hands press emptiness to my heart and it bruises my breast.*

13
Welcome To London

Our arrival in the UK in June 1970 was not quite what we had expected. Despite my not having seen my father for nine years and my mother for five, there was nobody to meet us at Heathrow Airport. Hardly the Prodigal's return!

Paddy had left her entire family behind and was feeling very low and anxious as she was coming into a new family she had never met. All she knew about them was from conversations with me or from their periodic letters to me. There was too, the anxiety and tiredness of travelling on a long flight with our baby son, Maric, who was 9 months old. We had given up everything to make a fresh start in the UK. We had our India Government allowance of £9 in cash but I had bought £50 on the black market in Calcutta and smuggled it out in my shoe—a serious offence which, had I been caught by the Indian authorities, would have probably landed me in jail.

Frantic phone calls from the airport to my parents' phone went unanswered. After a couple of hours it sank in that no one was coming to meet us so we asked around and were directed to the cheapest available transport in to London, the Airport bus, in the hope that we could try to contact the family there. To our immense relief we found the family waiting for us at Victoria Coach Station. It somehow hadn't occurred to them to go to the airport to meet us, or let us know what they planned to do!

Matters did not improve. On the way home, my parents admitted that the flat they had said so confidently that they would rent for us hadn't materialised, so we were to stay in one room in my brother Wensley's house until we could find somewhere of our own. He now had two young children, and was working for the tax department.

The next day I began to try to find work as quickly as possible as our smuggled money would not last long. A week later I started a job which I found through the vacancies in a London evening paper, as a Sales Order Clerk with a company that made beds in Vauxhall, central London, near the Oval cricket ground—fortunately only a short train ride away from where we were staying. It paid a very modest £19 a week, but I took home considerably less as I had to pay a third of it in 'emergency tax' until my proper tax code arrived, which would be in a few months. The job itself would have strained no one: salesmen phoned in orders for beds from stores around the country and I recorded them and passed the orders to the factory, which was across the road from us. It was tedious, but it was a start—and it improved my knowledge of English geography immensely.

Within a couple of months we had moved out of Wensley's house to a flat of our own in Battersea, just off the River Thames, secured through my parents' landlady—who took a shine to us. This was a stroke of luck as it was difficult to get accommodation to rent in London those days if you had children—landlords were notorious for putting notices in their windows advertising vacant flats but specifying, "No dogs, no children, no Blacks, no Irish".

Early Anglo-Indian migrants to England were often stunned to find that far from welcoming them, the British regarded them as 'Indians' and even questioned why they had left their country to come to live in England. Having mixed with the better class of Brit in India who attended the local dances, wooed the girls and played games of hockey and cricket with the men, they were faced with a population who knew little about Anglo-Indians and were suspicious of foreigners who spoke heavily accented sing-song English peppered with 'men' at the end of their sentences. Claims that they were British because they had English grandfathers were met with scorn—their colour often suggested to the locals that this was a doubtful story. Some then claimed Spanish, Portuguese or Italian ancestry to explain their colour and accents. A few, disillusioned, returned to India to resume their more comfortable lifestyles. Many of the immigrants took solace in getting together with fellow Anglo-Indians at dances and functions, exchanging experiences—and putting an over-positive spin on how they were faring in their new country and how much money they were making. They had found that Indian qualifications and trades experience counted for nothing and many took jobs on the railways or the buses or opted for low paid work mainly in the public services. I know of one middle aged senior executive from The Statesman who ended up as a postman. Any work was taken in order to gain a foothold in the country. And soon came the realisation that they might have to settle for being the stepping stones to a better future for their children—who, given the benefit of a British education, would become more integrated and would have greater opportunities to advance professionally and financially.

For many, including us, the first priority was to get somewhere decent to live. After our one-room existence it was nice to have a place of our own, even though it was two rooms in a draughty attic with an enclosed landing which functioned as a kitchen. The toilet, on the floor below, was shared with a widow in her 90s—stepping into her flat was like stepping back to the 1930s because of the old fashioned décor and the coal fired cast-iron cooking range. There was no bath so we had to make a weekly trip to the public 'slipper baths' down the road. A shilling gave access to a cubicle and a proper bath with plenty of hot water. It sounds Dickensian, but it was clean and comforting, I regarded it as a bit like a visit to the swimming pool.

Life was difficult on a small wage. At the end of the week, with careful housekeeping, we had coppers to spare. So I took on a Saturday job at a firm of men's outfitters—which also gave me discounts on clothes, which I badly needed. Before leaving India, I had asked my local tailor to make me several suits and overcoats but, unfortunately, he was working to a 1950s pattern book and I ended up dressed for post-World War II England! Remember that the 'swinging 60s' with its trendy Carnaby Street clothes was still going strong in London and the hippy revolution with even more colourful clothes was beginning—so I stood out even more.

Life in the little attic was tough for Paddy. Three flights of stairs to negotiate with a baby, no vacuum cleaner or washing machine (baby's terry-towel nappies were a problem to deal with, disposables hadn't been invented), and only a single electric ring to cook on and a single portable electric fire—both of which fed off a meter that hungrily gobbled up our meagre shillings. In winter the sharp wind coming off the River Thames howled through the gaps in the windows so we stuffed them with newspaper and marvelled at the sight of ice crystals forming inside the panes. And yes, of course, it snowed that Christmas for the first time in years. On the plus side, we had a rented black and white TV, quite a novelty for us, to which baby Maric became quite attached. He would stop whatever he was doing when the BBC 'spinning world' logo came on to signal the start of the next programme and dash to one of the two armchairs we had to sit in and wait to see what was on next. If it was of no interest, he went back to his play.

Paddy and Maric were on their own for six days a week while I worked at two jobs, so Sunday was our only free day together. We spent it either visiting my parents in Wimbledon, if we could afford the rail fare, or in walking around the nearby Battersea Park. We were too poor to do anything else. We were occasionally invited to visit Paddy's relatives in West London. This gave us a welcome respite—and it showed us what we could achieve as they were naturally keen to impress on us how well they were doing and to show off their houses and cars. But we also found it somewhat dispiriting as we were just scraping along.

Before leaving India, Desmond Doig had given me a letter of introduction to Sir William Collins, head of the Collins publishing empire. I made an appointment to see him and duly arrived, 'suited and booted' as we would have said in Calcutta, clutching a portfolio of my writing under my arm. I was ushered into the presence of the great man, who took Doig's letter and silently read it. He then pressed his intercom and asked a secretary to send in one of his managers. The chap arrived and Sir William said, "This is Thorpe, find a place for him in our outfit." I said my thanks and we left the office. When I got to the corridor outside I turned to the manager and said, "Thanks, but no thanks!" and walked off. I was incensed that Collins had not taken the trouble to find out more about me or to look at my work. While a job would have been nice, I was not prepared to take one under patronage.

In November 1970, five months after arriving in England, I passed the examinations and joined the British Civil Service as an Executive Officer working for the Department of Health and Social Security. The pay was better and the prospects infinitely more promising. At about the same time, the ground floor flat in our building became vacant and we moved into it. It was identical to my parents' flat—three rooms, a kitchen and bathroom—and there was also a small concrete courtyard with a war-time air-raid shelter in it. The move was just as well as our second child was on the way and we would need the extra space. A new life was beginning—in every sense of the word.

This is a story that will be familiar to many immigrants, most of whom faced hardship in their early years as they sought to establish a foothold in their new countries. I know of friends from India who took on a variety of low paid jobs—working as labourers, ticket collectors on the railways or London Underground, and even as fishermen on the prawn boats in Australia. Our Indian qualifications often counted for little and families, wives and girlfriends sometimes made heroic sacrifices, working hard and long hours while their husbands and boyfriends retook their qualifications—my wife's cousin worked hard as a secretary in Toronto while her husband re-took his qualifications as a dentist; the sacrifice was well worth it in the end. There was prejudice too. Our accents, and sometimes colour, marked us out as different—but we had been marked out as different in India anyway so it was nothing we couldn't handle.

14
What Happened Next?

So what did happen next? My parents continued life in their flat in Wimbledon. My mother had a local job with the telephone company, my father worked for London Underground doing a variety of jobs. He never ever complained about his loss of status and was cheerful and devil may care until, aged 79, he became slowly imprisoned by Parkinson's Disease, which robbed him of his emotions and his mobility, and finally his life. My mother remained sharp and critical to the end—right up to the day before she died, aged 84, of sheer old age. She always blamed my father for her change in fortune—never accepting that she had inadvertently played a part herself.

My brothers went on to have successful careers. Wensley became a tax inspector and retired early as Assistant Collector of Taxes in London to devote his time to his hobbies—woodcarving, golf and photography. He is still going strong. You can see his photographs of India if you Google his name, Wensley Thorpe (or Wes Thorpe), and find his website. John went into the Royal Navy after finishing school in the UK—a career choice largely made, I think, to escape from his family and be independent. He sailed the world, specialising in the electronic warfare computers on ships. He fought in the Falklands war of 1982, serving on the aircraft carrier HMS Hermes, which was the plum target for the Argentine pilots. After leaving the navy as a Chief Petty Officer he went to work for a series of defence companies, installing electronic warfare systems on warships and submarines—which he continues to do. Like a sailor, he has had some difficulty settling in to life on shore and has been through three marriages.

My sister Susan grew up, married a strange chap with Art Garfunkel hair who fancied himself as a rock singer, had a daughter, divorced, and worked for a telecommunications company before taking early retirement and going to live in Spain—joining a long line of

Brits chasing the sun.

And me? I prospered in the Civil Service and finally retired in March 2006 as a senior civil servant in one of the major Government departments dealing with social security and unemployment.

In the course of my work in Government I got into the 'fast stream', which was the route to quick advancement, competing with undergraduates from Oxford and Cambridge. I served as Private Secretary to Ministers in both the Labour and Conservative administrations (when Mrs Thatcher became Prime Minister). I was part of the group that in 1978 investigated the last smallpox outbreak in the UK (currently in the world); I worked in the European Community in Brussels, negotiating on behalf of the UK on social security issues; was briefly a Consultant in Eastern Europe advising countries in the post-Communist era on the reconstruction of their social security systems, and was responsible for setting up two new organisations for the UK Government—the Independent Social Security Appeals Service and the Child Support Agency– the latter has been very controversial. I also led work to computerise the largest Government department, the Department for Social Security. In the course of my career I formulated policy and supported Ministers in Parliament—feeding them with briefing and answers to queries during Parliamentary debates—passing chits to the Government Whips to give to them. I'd sometimes sit there as Parliament droned on thinking, "We come from two quite completely different worlds, you and me. How did I go from running about barefoot, being able to fire a catty, cut a kite and take a chip of wood off a spinning top to writing speeches for Ministers of the British Crown!"

I cannot write in detail about these experiences without seeking Government permission as I am bound, as all UK civil servants are, by the Official Secrets Act. Working in Government has been a hoot at times so I can understand why Ministers and senior officials might not be keen on the publicity.

Being a chokra in the 'magic circle' of the senior civil service, known to the British press and public as the Mandarins (not a complimentary term, by the way), has been interesting. I have never made a secret of being Anglo-Indian and have never encountered direct discrimination or overt racism. However, that is not to say there has never been discrimination—just perhaps that it has been more subtle, and I have had to work very hard to over-perform in order to achieve success. I made many good friends and take away very special memories—and can point to many achievements. Whether I would have had the same level of success in India is debatable. England has also made me a more rounded person, able to undertake a variety of do-it-yourself, mechanical and manual tasks—I like getting my hands dirty! And books and art are my passions.

Paddy too went to work for Government, moving from working on social security to dealing with flood defences—the British coastline is steadily eroding in places, and the increase in building homes on river flood plains has, predictably, led to increases in the number of floods in rainy England. She recently retired and hopes to spend more time in her garden and in seeing the world with me.

And I discovered my roots!

With the advance of the Internet it became easier for families to begin to try to trace their origins. My grandfather, Horace Langridge, had run away from his family, and a stepfather, who I presume he didn't like, to join the army, the Sussex Regiment, and go overseas to India so avoiding ending up as just another agricultural labourer in Sussex. He adopted his step-father's surname, Thorpe. He never returned from India—having acquired a wife and several children I don't suppose he could afford to. My father only had a sketchy knowledge of where his family came from—the Parish of Maresfield in East Sussex. In the early 2000s, using the internet and census records we were able to pinpoint his home in the village of Fletching, East Sussex.

We visited Fletching, a beautiful old village with a wonderful old pub called the Griffin. We were able to see the cottage where my grandfather had grown up, and to visit the graves of our ancestors in the local churchyards. It was a very strange feeling for me to suddenly know that I had roots and to know where I had come from. As an Anglo-Indian in India I had felt somewhat stateless, in a sort of limbo. Now I could touch the font in the church where my grandfather and his mother were baptised, and I could read my family name on the tombstones and know that my family had walked these streets and probably drunk in the Griffin for generations. It was an indescribable feeling of belonging.

I resolved to know more about my family. The Langridge clan lived around the East Grinstead, Uckfield, and Fletching areas of Sussex for a long time. My grandfather's people were agricultural labourers. In India, my grandfather, Horace, met and married Minna Evans, about whose family I know absolutely nothing, and produced four sons: Leonard, who worked in accounts and who died in England in the 1970s; Eric, my father; Owen, Lieutenant in the 3/17 Dogra Regiment, who was killed in Singapore; and Richard, who was a doctor (anaesthetist) in the Indian Army, and who died in the late 1960s in the week I was due to go and meet him for the first time. Grandfather Horace eventually left the army and joined the railways as a guard/ticket collector, working in Rawalpindi—then in India but now part of Pakistan.

Further research has established that I can tentatively (and I say that because it is based on somebody else's research) trace my family through my father's family line to 1247 and the appointment of a member of our Langridge family, then spelt Da Lyngrigge, as sergeant forester in Ashdown Forest in Sussex, later the setting for the Winnie the Pooh stories. Given the French name, it is possible that the family were part of the Norman invasion of Britain in 1066, but that link has yet to be proven. A later ancestor, Sir Edward Dallingridge (note how the spelling has changed[1]) fought in France in the 1300s in the Hundred Years' War alongside King Edward III and his son, the Black Prince, and also went on to suppress the Welsh rebellion and conquer Wales. By all accounts he was a character—he even challenged Prince John of Gaunt, one of the King's other sons, to a duel to settle a land dispute. He was briefly Lord Mayor of London in 1392. But his enduring legacy is that he built the beautiful Bodiam Castle in East Sussex in 1385—it still stands, though the inside is a ruin. Unfortunately, the Langridge family eventually sold it so there is no prospect of turn-

---

1   because we were at war with the French, the old Norman names were being anglicised.

ing at the castle gates and staking a claim.

In 2005, Paddy and I had our DNA sampled by a firm called Oxford Ancestors, part of Oxford University (e-mail www.oxfordancestors.com if you want to do yours). Their research on DNA has enabled them to establish people's pre-historic origins. We had our genetic roots traced through the maternal line using mitochondrial DNA. This is present in every cell in our bodies and is passed on exclusively through our mothers, and is therefore able to pinpoint our genetic legacy. Research at Oxford has suggested that everyone on Earth is descended from one of only 36 'clan mothers'.

Paddy's DNA was traced back 25,000 years to a clan that lived on the cold and inhospitable European tundra at the eastern edge of the Black Sea. As the climate grew worse with the onset of the last Ice Age, the clan left the rapidly cooling mountains and spread out to the east and west. They were prodigious travellers and descendants can be found all over Europe but also, intriguingly, among the Native American Indian tribes in North America. This means that a few members of the clan must have travelled right across Asia and joined the first expeditions across the then dry Bering land bridge into the Americas. Given Paddy's Malay Chinese background, her ancestors must have given the land bridge a miss, and been among those who moved East across Central Asia and Siberia into China, then much later migrated into Malaysia.

My DNA was traced back 45,000 years to a clan that lived in what is now northern Greece. They were among the first arrivals of a new, modern human to set foot in Europe who began to displace the Neanderthals. They spread right across Europe, west across France and north as far as the British Isles. As the climate deteriorated 25,000 years ago with the dawning of yet another Ice Age, they moved south, eventually reaching Spain, which became a refuge for humans fleeing the cold. As the climate warmed they moved back north. They reached the British Isles—and left an indelible record in the limestone caves of Cheddar Gorge in Somerset. It turns out that they may have been cannibals...

My two children, Maric and Paul, consider themselves to be English, but are also keenly aware of their Anglo-Indian background. Maric is a doctor who heads the Accident and Emergency service in the Isle of Man—where he is kept very busy patching up casualties from the annual TT motorcycle races. Paul works as a project manger for a computer company but his passion is creating and playing music. He currently has a band called The Voodoo Trombone Quartet who have had good reviews. Though it is called a quartet there are seven players—because Paul created the original music on his own and was then persuaded to form a band to play it (Google

'Voodoo Trombone Quartet' to hear their music).

Paddy and I also have four grandchildren, Natasha, Oscar, Albert and Daisy. They are too little to know about their Anglo-Indian history but we will tell them about it when they get older. And, like small Anglo-Indians everywhere, the older ones already love a good curry!

> I must launch out my boat. The languid hours pass by on the shore—Alas for me!
>
> The spring has done its flowering and taken leave. And now with the burden of faded futile flowers I wait and linger.
>
> The waves have become clamorous, and upon the bank in the shady lane the yellow leaves flutter and fall.
>
> What emptiness do you gaze upon! Do you not feel a thrill passing through the air with the notes of the far away song floating from the other shore?
>
> Tagore—Gitanjali

Now turn to the next page to read The Tree—a Monsoon short story.

APPENDIX A

The Tree

A Monsoon short story—first published in the Junior Statesman Magazine in 1969.

Sleepily Anant Rao hoisted the last of the bedding out of the compartment and looked at his watch—1.30 a.m. Four and a half hours to go before they could get any conveyance to take them to the farm. The whistle of the train sliced through the cold night air and with a clatter the long serrated hulk crept out of the station. Anant Rao watched it disappear into the black, mist-shrouded night, then herded Vijaya and little Rani into the waiting room to catch some sleep.

The bench was hard. He pondered on these new discomforts. Trains that stopped at stations at ungodly hours and hard benches with bugs. Was he doing the right thing in coming out to Sonagram to work the fields his uncle had bequeathed him? He had never even seen the place, but visions of a life of a man of property and plenty were temptations enough to resign the Government clerical post he had held—and hated.

Vijaya had silently accepted her lot but Rani's four-year-old mind had wandered into ecstasies over stories of rural pleasures. And she couldn't wait to come to grips with this delightful new world.

A cartman sat under a tree sipping a morning mug of tea. "Will you take me to Sonagram?" asked Anant Rao, "and my family? There is also some luggage." "In a minute," said the cartman, "but you are new here and I know everybody in Sonagram, I'm from there myself. And nobody is expecting relatives."

"Oh, nobody knows we're coming", replied Anant Rao, "as a matter of fact, I own land over there and we are going to live on it."

"I know everyone who owns land in Sonagram", said the cartman, "but I don't know you."

"How could you?" laughed the other. "I was left the land by my uncle, Bhaskar Rao."

"Bhaskar!", shouted the cartman, "you are going to live on Bhaskar Rao's land? Are you mad? Don't you know?"

"What's wrong?", cried Anant Rao.

But the cartman remained mum, his eyes fixed on the trees. Finally, he looked at Anant Rao with compassion and said, "Bhai, go back to where you came from. You do not know the ways of the land and this land is not lucky. In fact Bhaskar Rao's plot has never produced well and there is always drought in summer. Go back."

"No," said Anant Rao perplexed. "And what is wrong with the place—tell me."

"I am pleading with you Bhai, go back. I advise you as a son. This is a hard place and you have a young wife and a child."

"Take me to Sonagram," commanded Anant Rao.

Bhola, the cartman, stopped his bullock cart after crossing a rise and pointed to a path that disappeared between dense trees. "That is the way to your new property. Go and see, I will wait for you here with your wife and your child and your luggage in case you want me to take you back to the station."

Stepping through the trees Anant Rao came upon a stretch of flat, cleared land—fields that were overrun with grass and weeds. "Why, the liar," he thought as his eyes roved over his domain with its rich fertility. The grass grew thick and lush, with flowers of yellow and of blue peering over the blades. The outlines of the bunds were still discernible and Anant Rao reckoned he could make things ship-shape with a few weeks of hard work.

The sound of crows cawing drew him towards a thicket in the middle of the furthest field. Soon he made out the vague outlines of a house between the trees. Stepping through the glade he came into a large clearing and his heart sank at the crumbling ruins of what was once a stout dwelling. The roof was intact but there were gaping holes in the walls and grass grew all over the floor.

Anant Rao stepped round to the back of the house after inspecting every room. In bad condition but liveable, he thought. But plenty of work to do. At the back there was a disused tube-well, now covered with weeds, and behind it a magnificent banyan tree in fruit. Its long straight pillars of aerial roots formed a dense ring round the thick trunk and a scattering of ripe red berries lay around. Its size and perfection awed Anant Rao. Vijaya could set up a small temple here for her family deity. The place would be perfect.

Quietly a gloom seemed to steal over the glade. And Anant Rao felt a chill creep through the trees. The cawing of the crows was stilled. Anant Rao glanced uneasily around. The house had taken on an ethereal glow and the gashes of the windows were penetrating eyes. He listened for any sound but even the chirping of the crickets had been stilled. Then Anant Rao swung round to face the tree. The long roots seemed menacing and the shadows seemed to harbour evil. Anant Rao fought a desire to run and sweat stood out on his forehead. Evil. There was something evil here and the cartman had feared something. He had glimpsed the terror in his eyes.

Then the moment passed and the sounds of nature crowded on his ears. Sunlight slatted through the trees and the banyan had assumed its kind benevolence. Anant Rao trudged back chiding himself for his nervousness. Only a cloud passing over the sun and I get so scared he thought. All for nothing. But deep down he could not explain that moment of malevolence which had engulfed him. These damn villagers and their tales. They probably wanted the fields for themselves.

Winter passed and Anant Rao and his family had settled into the house beside the banyan. The fields had been tilled and now cows chewed the cud in a new barn and chickens scampered round the backyard scratching the soil for food. Anant Rao had even acquired a degree of acceptance by the villagers of Sonagram. Chandgi Ram, the headman, and Govind Rao, the purohit, were his friends and he visited them whenever he took the two furlong walk to the village.

Through the good offices of Bahuraj, the moneylender, he had secured the services of Natesa, a middle aged grouch with a heart of gold who helped him in the fields.

Anant Rao was happy, except for certain moments when he was working in the compound of his house and the same malevolent gloom seemed to oppress the place and then lift as abruptly as it came.

Summer came, but no rain. The fields were parched and the soil turned a burnt khaki shade. Heat waves shimmered over burnished stones and eyes anxiously turned towards the sky.

"Is it always like this, purohit?" asked Anant Rao.

"The rains will break soon," replied the purohit.

"I'll be glad when that happens," said Anant Rao, "I don't want the first crop to fail and my cattle to die."

"Anant Rao, there is something I must tell you."

"Yes?"

"Go away for the summer; it will be bad for you. Your place—it is evil."

"So, you too knew," said Anant Rao. "I have felt that way often, but nobody seems to want to explain things. What's the big secret?"

"The secret is in the tree," replied the purohit.

"The banyan?"

"Yes, don't let anyone near the banyan in summer."

Coming across the fields, Anant Rao stopped to survey the glade. Something seemed strange. He could not fathom it. Something was out of place. He passed Natesa sitting outside his hut and stopped to chat.

"Natesa bhai," "I was looking at the glade and something seems to be inconsistent. Do have a look yourself."

"The Tree," said Natesa quietly without looking up.

"The Tree. By God you're right! It's incredible. Every plant and tree in the whole State is shrivelled and dry, but that banyan gleams as though after the first rains. The leaves, look Natesa, the leaves are green. It's unbelievable."

"It's worse than that," said Natesa. "Babu—I would like to go away to my brother's village across the river to stay there till the drought is over. We can't do any work here now. Why don't you come too?"

"No," replied Anant Rao. "You go, leave tomorrow morning, if you like. You're right, we can do nothing till the rains come."

Anant Rao couldn't sleep. The night was too still and warm. He rose from his charpoy for a drink of water—when he heard the soft crackle of dry leaves being trod. He froze. Then he peered out of the window. The pallid moonlight bathed the banyan and the glade. Even as he watched, the sound grew closer. Measured steps. A cloud began to obscure the moon and shadows rushed to hold the glade fast in a web of black. Through the darkness Anant Rao could hear the footsteps approaching and then he felt the presence of evil creep out of the banyan and radiate across the glade. A magnetic pull of high intensity.

The steps went by and yet Anant Rao saw no figure. His hair stood on end. The steps were going towards the banyan—there was the sudden crack of a whiplash followed by a raucous scream. Anant Rao's knees gave way and he tried to shout, but in vain. Silence descended but the evil seemed to linger and its oppressive presence suffocated him.

In the morning they found Natesa dangling from one of the tendrils of the banyan, his neck encircled by its fleshy pink coils. In the afternoon the rain fell.

"Purohit, he wasn't drunk and he wasn't unhappy," said Anant Rao, "why did he do it?"

"So you still think Natesa hanged himself," asked the purohit.

"Wait! I remember the sound of a whiplash—perhaps there was a breeze that blew the roots around his neck and in the dark he tripped!"

"There was no breeze."

"Then how...?"

"The tree, Anant Rao," said the purohit quietly. "The tree is cursed. Every drought this happens. The tree remains the only green thing around for miles. People get drawn to it and --- and they fall prey to its clutches."

"What?" exclaimed Anant Rao. "Ridiculous!"

"Then the rain falls," said the purohit. "When the tree is satisfied."

"It's impossible," said Anant Rao. "Natesa knew about the tree, why did he go to it late at night if he was aware of the risks?"

"He did not want to go," replied the purohit. "He had to go. The tree beckoned."

"You are a man of the scriptures, purohit," said Anant Rao. "Is all this logical?"

"Is Hanuman logical? Is God logical?" asked the purohit. "The banyan is a holy tree. There is a story that the Creator dropped one seed on this world at the dawn of creation. That seed multiplied and spread its roots all over this earth. The roots became individual trees, natural temples where man could attain peace of mind and serve God. They are all linked—all banyans. One is the father of the other."

"Yes—that's all right. But this tree seems evil. Is God evil? Explain that!"

"There has been a sin upon this tree," said the purohit. "Ask Chandgi Ram, the headman, he will know the story better. He has been here longer."

Chandgi Ram drew on his ganja pipe. "Long ago," he said, "a yogi lived under that tree. And every year the villagers would make offerings to him and he would appeal to the Almighty on behalf of the villagers for good crops. One year there was a drought. Everything died. Except the banyan. The villagers approached the yogi but he could do nothing. Someone spread a story that he was a fake. So they hung him from his own tree. Those were bad years."

"What then?", asked Anant Rao.

"Since then the tree has avenged itself on the villagers," said Chandgi Ram. "Many have paid the price of folly. After the sacrifice the tree is satisfied. God's revenge is terrible."

Winter passed into spring. Then again the terrible drought. But Anant Rao's tree remained green and fresh. The villagers tried persistently to persuade him to leave but he refused. He bought a gun instead and had a carpenter come from Maithili, ten miles away, to make the doors and windows strong and fast. He forbade Vijaya and Rani to go near the tree until after the rains.

One night he retired with an uneasy feeling of impending disaster. The tree had seemed more malevolent than ever and the glade had lapsed into silence.

Around midnight Anant Rao woke suddenly sensing something wrong. He listened. There was a soft click and the squeak of slowly opening door. Grabbing his gun he rushed to the front door and found it wide open. There was nobody there!

Shakily Anant Rao bolted the door and awoke Vijaya. "There are dacoits here," he said, "be watchful."

Presently, against the ticking of the clock he heard the

sound again. A soft click, then a squeak. Anant Rao was up. The moon had been obscured. He could only see the faint outlines of the evil banyan.

"Vijaya, get up," he said. Then he tiptoed to the front door and…it was wide open. The latch had been lifted from inside! Anant Rao felt his scalp prickle and peered about the dark room, his gun at the ready.

Then… there was a choking gasp followed by a scream.

Anant Rao dashed into the bedroom to find Vijaya screaming hysterically and pointing to the window. It was open—from the inside—and…Rani had gone.

Shouting, Anant Rao charged outside into the back compound towards the tree. There was a blinding flash and sheets of rain poured down on him obscuring his view and beating him back relentlessly. He had never felt rain so powerful. It seemed to push him with an unseen hand. Even the earth began to tremble.

Anant Rao could not give up and fought his way to the banyan. There was a crack and he saw the falling bough too late.

Vijaya found him next morning, dazed but alive. Together they sobbed at the sight of a pale pink frock dangling forty feet from the ground. The legs that protruded from it were lifeless. The neck was broken and lovingly entwined in the fleshy tendrils of the tree.

The next week Anant Rao called two men from the city. Diehards, who would do anything for money. And they chopped at the tree. Root by root till they came to the main trunk. Anant Rao personally took the axe, watched from a distance by the villagers in fear and trepidation. He hacked and cut at the knotted wood till it fell with a resounding crash into the glade. The villagers shied away, muttering prayers. The purohit said quietly, "God protect us now. We need it."

After the tree had fallen Anant Rao poured kerosene over the wood and set fire to it. The flames rose high into the air, so high that the villagers of Maithili could see them.

He said goodbye to the villagers, who remained sullen and silent. A few even suggested stoning him. The purohit and the headman refused to have anything to do with him and he turned sadly away to begin the trek to the station in the dying sunlight with his two labourers and his sobbing wife.

There was a brief search for a job in the city and Anant Rao went back to clerking. He tried in vain to sell his land in Sonagram as prospective buyers met with stern resistance from the villagers when they went to inspect the land. Meanwhile, he took lodgings in a dingy little room off the city's main street, among the dirt and the drains.

Winter gave way to spring, and spring to summer—

and Anant Rao remembered the drought of Sonagram. Even the city was dry this year and the newspaper said this was likely to continue. He trudged uneasily down the crowded street on his way home. Vijaya would be doing her puja when he got there. She had become very religious and very nervous since Rani's death.

That night Anant Rao lay in his charpoy listening to his wife's steady breathing. Exactly a year ago Rani had died. But the tree was no more. The few reports he had had from Sonagram had not indicated any undue trouble. There was absolutely no sign of life on the charred circle that had once been the tree. But that was a thing of the past. He lay in the dark in the cluttered room with its peeling walls.

Slowly he became aware of a faint slithering sound— like a snake, under his bed. He jumped up and grabbed a stick. But there was nothing there. "I'm jumpy," he thought uneasily as he bolted the windows.

Then he felt something creeping along his bed. He lay still in numbed fear. He opened his mouth to call Vijaya but no sound came. Reaching desperately for the torch under his pillow he fumbled for the switch. Beads of sweat popped out of his skin and his hackles rose. The slithering came closer and closer. Anant Rao couldn't move. Finally, with a supreme effort of will he flashed on the torch...

The pink fleshy tendril seemed to stare at him as it crept slowly, inexorably towards his pillow.

And the purohit's words coursed through his mind... "One banyan is the father of the other."

A large crowd gathered under a banyan tree in Bihardas Lane, just off the main road, to look at the unknown man hanging limply from its tendrils. Forty feet high. How did he manage to get there? Why did he do it? It was a good day for theories.

And it rained in Sonagram.

APPENDIX B

A Selection Of Suggested Reading

If you want to know more about Anglo-Indians and life in Anglo-India there are numerous books around. Here are a few interesting ones:

Britain's Betrayal in India: the Story of the Anglo-Indians—Frank Anthony. Published 1969, Allied Publishers, Bombay.

These are the Anglo-Indians—Reginald Maher. 1962, Swallow Press, Calcutta.

Under the Old School Topee—Hazel Innes Craig. 1990 by BACSA

Growing up in Anglo-India—Eric Stracey. 2000 by EastWest Books, Chennai

1600-1947 Anglo-Indian Legacy—Alfred D. F. (George) Gabb. 1998, Quacks Books.

India Britannica—Geoffrey Moorhouse. 1983, Paladin Books

Calcutta Past and Present—Kathleen Bletchynden. 1905, W. Thacker & Co.

Calcutta, the City Revealed—Geoffrey Moorhouse. 1974, Penguin Books.

Hobson-Jobson, the Anglo-Indian Dictionary—first published 1886 but still in print from Wordsworth Reference.

Kim—Rudyard Kipling. Penguin Books

Gitanjali—Rabindranath Tagore. 1913, Macmillan & Co.

The Jadu House, Intimate Histories of Anglo-India—Laura Roychowdhury. 2000, Doubleday.

Sikander Sahib—The Life of Colonel James Skinner 1778-1841—Dennis Holman. Published Heinemann 1961.

An Indian Affair, from Riches to Raj—Archie Baron. 2001

ISBN 142512965-X